Getting Your Message Across

Getting Your Message Across

Kathlyn Gay

A Skillbook

New Discovery Books
New York

Maxwell Macmillan Canada
Toronto

Maxwell Macmillan International
New York · Oxford · Singapore · Sydney

Book design: Deborah Fillion

New Discovery Books
Macmillan Publishing Company
866 Third Avenue
New York, NY 10022

Maxwell Macmillan Canada, Inc.
1200 Eglinton Avenue East
Suite 200
Don Mills, Ontario M3C 3N1

Macmillan Publishing Company is part of the Maxwell
Communication Group of Companies.

First edition

Printed in the United States of America

10 9 8 7 6 5 4 3 2 1

Library of Congress Cataloging-in-Publication Data
Gay, Kathlyn.
    Getting your message across / by Kathlyn Gay. — 1st ed.
       p. cm.
    Includes bibliographical references.
    Summary: A guide to effective communication, through
speaking, writing, appearance, and body language, with a look at
various obstacles to clear presentation.
    ISBN 0-02-735815-1
    1. Communication—Juvenile literature. [1. Communication.]
I. Title.
P91.2.G38 1993
302.2—dc20   92-41820

Contents

Chapter One

How People Communicate

"Read my lips! No new taxes," said candidate George Bush during his 1988 presidential campaign when asked repeatedly if he planned to increase federal taxes. The public picked up on the read-my-lips phrase as a way to repeat and emphasize many types of messages. However, taxes increased during Bush's presidency, so the meaning of the famous phrase changed. Now some people use it in a cynical fashion to warn that words may *not* mean what they say.

Although few of us are elected to public office, we all face times when we must be accountable for the messages we deliver. In addition, we all depend on a mixture of techniques to express our needs, wants, ideas, and opinions. You might convey messages in verbal form—in spoken or written words that are symbols for thoughts and ideas. But language, or the use of words, is only a small part of the communication process. According to anthropologist Edward T. Hall, a pioneer in the study of nonverbal communication, research shows that "80 to 90 percent of information is communicated by other means."[1]

Verbal and Nonverbal Messages

People frequently take for granted the many forms as well as means of communication, because most are part of daily routine. From a wake-up call or alarm in the morning to a good-night-sleep-well wish, we receive or send messages in verbal or nonverbal form all day long.

Perhaps you begin a day by jotting down a list of "things to do" in a notebook or on a chalkboard or type it into a computer program.

Maybe one of your tasks is to telephone a dozen people to invite them to a party. Several times you try to reach a person and cannot, so you may leave a message on an answering machine or decide to send your invitation by mail.

You might write a thank-you note to a relative who has sent you a gift.

You might go to a class, or attend a meeting and listen to a speaker, and then raise your hand to respond to a question or to participate in a discussion.

You might listen to someone tell a funny story and laugh and comment in response.

You might sit in a public park with a friend sharing events of the day and during the conversation see an acquaintance pass by—you wave a greeting.

Writing, talking, listening, providing feedback (responses) to another speaker, and vocalizing—using sounds such as "mmhm," or "hmph!" or "ew-eeeee!" or cries and moans—are all part of the communication process. So are body movements, often called body language, and gestures.

Even the space around you can be part of a message. For example, if you sit on a bench in a public place, you might mark the space beside you with a package or books to indicate that you want to reserve some distance between yourself and whoever else might sit down. In effect, you are marking your territory and telling strangers not to get too close.

Manner of dress—what people wear—may impart a message as well. Various uniforms help identify a mail carrier, police officer, delivery person, nurse, park ranger, baseball player, and many other kinds of professionals. People also wear clothing and accessories that convey such messages as "I'm part of the group" or "I'm exclusive" or "I don't want to be noticed too much" or "Look at me—I'm original!"

Changes in Means of Communication

Along with the vocal sounds and verbal and nonverbal forms of communication, people use varied mechanical means to deliver messages. These have changed drastically over the centuries.

Many thousands of years ago information conveyed vocally was the primary means of delivering messages. As people formed communities and villages and built cities, word-of-mouth communication continued to be one of the most important means of imparting information and ideas. This is true even today in some parts of the world.

In early villages and cities, street criers made public announcements, spread news, or advertised goods and services. Hawkers, for example, advertised goods for sale, ranging from cattle to wine.

Ancient people also used a written medium, carving hieroglyphs, or picture symbols, into stone walls and monuments and writing on papyrus, a form of paper made from papyrus reeds. Yet hieroglyphs were not the most effective means of putting across messages, because only a few people knew how to decipher the written language. So public places frequently were identified with symbols. For example, a picture of a goat symbolized a dairy, and a bush was a sign for the wine maker. A sign showing a boy being whipped marked a school. The symbol represented the kind of discipline used to enforce learning and also the fact that only boys were formally educated—girls were not allowed to attend school.

City or courtyard walls or the outside of public buildings were a medium for communication. In ancient Rome, for example, walls were usually whitewashed and then filled with pictures and symbols. Perhaps the message announced a play, circus, or a freshwater bath.[2]

Although the written word became a popular and effective form of communication, it almost disappeared after the Roman Empire collapsed, in A.D. 476. Conquerors who dominated Rome for many centuries did not value literacy, so for nearly 1,000 years few advances were made in the ways and means of spreading information or educating people.

But between the 1300s and 1600s trade and industry began to rebound again. With economic advances in Europe came better living standards, and the levels of education and literacy rose. Publishers began to produce the forerunner of the newspaper—newsbooks, which were booklets or pamphlets filled with news. However, the newsbooks did not contain current information as we might expect today. Rather, the information was compiled and published only once a year or every two or three years.

Communication Media Today

Today instant news is available. Publishers can print materials and distribute them within a few minutes, hours, days, or weeks. Billboards, placards, posters, and many types of clothing from caps to T-shirts are imprinted with words and symbols designed to send a message. Even video games carry special slogans. The United States Environmental Protection Agency and the American Amusement Machine Association recently joined forces to promote the idea of recycling solid waste materials by incorporating the message "Recycle, Don't Trash It!" on the screens of various video games.

Telephones, video and audio tapes, photographs, and films are other means of rapidly transmitting information and ideas. So are automated banking tellers and ticket vendors. The machines ask questions and accept coded responses on an electronic screen to make transactions.

Radio, television, the Teletype, and fax machines transmit messages across a nation or around the world in minutes. In Australia, for example, radio communication is vital to an educational program called School of the Air. The school employs 240 teachers who, via radio hookups, instruct more than 2,500 students, ranging from preschool to seventh grade. Teachers send assignments through the mail or by fax machines. In most cases, students live on remote ranches, hours from the nearest town and so far from schools that daily transportation back and forth is not practical. Similar long-distance education also is conducted in Canada and Wales.[3]

With the use of satellites, video conferencing allows people from different parts of the world or outer space to talk to one another "face-to-face" on television hookups. Messages also can be shared globally through computers and modems connected to various electronic conferences, bulletin boards, and mail services.

The Importance of Personal Communication Skills

Throughout history, people have attained leadership and sometimes great power and influence because they could effectively put across their views and motivate others to act. Effective communication is also important in countless jobs and professions. But businesspeople say large numbers of applicants cannot be hired because they lack communication skills. In its 1991 survey of 400 manufacturing firms, the National Association of Manufacturers found that although companies rejected applicants for multiple reasons, 37 percent were turned away because of poor reading and writing skills and 25 percent were rejected because of poor speaking skills.[4]

Many employers and educators say that written and oral communication skills and the ability to transfer information will be vital for most future jobs. In fact, companies and organizations have been established to teach employees basic skills. One nonprofit firm in Washington, D.C., called Language at Work, has been expanding its operations ever since it was set up in 1985. "More and more employers are becoming aware that to train valued present employees is a better financial investment than hiring new ones," according to Vera Dickey, one of the founders.[5]

Communication skills are vital for people in such professions as engineering, publishing, law, medicine, science, and teaching. People who provide many types of services, ranging from an airline pilot to hotel front desk clerk to zoo guide, cannot perform their jobs well if they cannot communicate information. People in business management, in the clergy, medicine, teaching, and many other careers need speech and writing skills to instruct and communicate with others.

Along with the workplace, there are other settings in which communication is important, such as in family life, in relationships with friends, in social activities, in schools, and in the marketplace. Communication is also an integral part of the creative arts, from dance to drama. But artistic expression is not within the scope of this book. Instead, the focus is on how people apply communication skills and convey messages within varied contexts, including guidelines on how you can effectively transmit ideas, wants, and needs and understand the messages of others.

Chapter Two

More Than Talk

"Talk, talk, talk." You've probably heard people grumble about folks who babble onandonandon, in motor-mouth fashion for what can seem like hours. Perhaps you know or have encountered a nonstop talker who ignores your attempts to be part of a conversation, never pausing long enough for you to contribute your ideas. Obviously if only one person has the opportunity to speak, no real dialogue takes place. Instead the sole talker delivers a monologue or even a lecture, and only one person has the opportunity to express ideas or views.

A monologue is one form of speech communication. TV hosts frequently open talk and variety shows with a monologue, and teachers usually begin classes with uninterrupted discourse. Other types of uninterrupted speech include a sales presentation, formal lecture, and sermon.

The most common form of speech communication is conversation between two people—face-to-face or by telephone—or group discussion with several people taking part. Conversations and discussions can be personal—such as between friends or family members, or impersonal—as in conversation with a salesperson or a discussion among classmates or co-workers.

No matter what its form, speech communication includes not only words but also what experts call paralanguage—messages delivered with vocal signals such as groans, sighs, and coughs. One's speech pattern (slow or fast pace), tone of voice, and the emphasis placed on words are also components of paralanguage. Any one or all of them can affect the meaning of what you say. You can test this by repeating a sentence, putting emphasis on a different word each time to change the meaning:

I **drove the new car.**

 (suggesting that no one else drove)

I drove the *new* car.

(suggesting there is an older car available)

I drove the new *car*.

(suggesting there is another new vehicle—perhaps
a truck—available)

A speaker's body language and verbal and nonverbal feedback from others are also important components of speech communication. These are discussed in more detail later, but the point is that the meaning of a spoken message frequently depends on much more than the talk you hear.

Manner of Speaking

In infancy a person begins to learn a manner of speaking by mimicking adult sounds and, later, speech patterns. If your vocal sounds and words are understood, you generally do not give much thought to your speaking habits. But you might become aware of speech patterns if your or someone else's manner of speaking seems to inhibit com-

munication in situations such as applying for a job or trying to persuade others to take action.

Some speech patterns can irritate and block communication. For example, few people want to listen to mumblers,
whiners, or shouters. It is not unusual for people to switch
off a TV or radio station if a speaker's voice grates, such as
when a salesperson bellows out a commercial for used cars
or other products. Listeners may also tune out a person
with a high-pitched, squeaky voice that sets up barriers for
the listener. Clipped, sarcastic tones also can be a turnoff
if used consistently in everyday conversation or in a formal
speech.

A flat monotone can put people to sleep. Sometimes a
person who speaks in such a manner is labeled a bore. Researchers have identified a number of other traits that mark
a boring speaker. They include talking only about oneself,
complaining about problems, being overly serious, lacking
enthusiasm, and continually conforming to others' views
rather than expressing one's own opinion.[1]

Even though people learn and develop their speech patterns from infancy on, those habits can be changed. But
why would anyone want to learn new patterns unless her
or his livelihood depended on being a skillful communicator? One answer is that a calm, pleasant, easy-on-the-ears
voice can be an asset in many situations where you want
to convey or receive messages.

Perhaps you use the telephone to obtain information or
to request a special favor. Your manner of speaking may
determine whether you succeed. A person on the other end
is likely to make a judgment about you just from your voice.
If you come across as self-assured, polite, and pleasantly
persuasive, then chances are your request will be granted.

A demanding, gruff, and overbearing voice may have just the opposite effect.

Some people who want to improve their speech mannerisms may enroll in speech and diction classes, use self-help audio tapes on the subject, or take part in school or civic theater productions. Another common method for developing effective speech patterns is to record your voice with a tape recorder and play it back to note habits that might interfere with what you have to say. For a recording you can read a favorite story or poem, parts from a play, or a famous speech. You can also record a family conversation or a chat with a friend—with permission, of course.

When you listen to a recording of your voice, you can identify such problems as slurred speech or vocalized pauses such as "uh," "er," "anduh," or repeated and irritating (to the listener) phrases such as "you know" or "I mean."

In face-to-face conversations, you can determine whether you deliver your words in a clear and pleasant manner by watching for nonverbal feedback and by listening to the way others respond to your words. Suppose you have to explain to someone how to do a class assignment or tasks on a job. Maybe you speak so fast that the other person has to interrupt to ask questions in order to grasp all that you say. Or you might speak so slowly that a listener becomes impatient and begins to daydream or think about other things while you speak.

Perhaps you send a know-it-all message with your tone of voice. Or you could give the impression that you are unsure of what you say. If the other person constantly fidgets, frowns, turns aside, or exhibits other behavior that seems to say "I'm tuning you out," then you may want to check your speaking manner.

There are many different speech patterns that can detract from or be a barrier to communication. But if you listen carefully to your own voice and become aware of the speech patterns you use, you are taking a step toward making positive changes. You can also practice clear speech—pronouncing words so that they can be understood—and getting to the point of your message without side trips into irrelevant territory.

Another helpful measure is to find a critic to work with you to identify and change distracting speech patterns. An objective helper might also call attention to nonverbal messages that can obstruct speech communication.

Not by Words Alone

Most people are not aware in formal speechmaking or in informal one-to-one conversations that, along with paralanguage, other types of nonverbal messages accompany the words they speak. Consider a few brief examples:

- A park director escorts visitors through a new recreational facility, stopping at various activity areas to explain what's going on. Whenever the director talks, he holds his hands up under his chin, palms crossed, rubbing his hands in a back and forth motion. Watching him, listeners are not only distracted by the hand movements but also interpret them to mean that the director is arrogant, condescending to all around him. The palm rubbing suggests a kind of calculating, greedy individual.

- A group of young people is gathered around a table discussing ways to raise funds for an environmental project. All participants are leaning forward, some with elbows on the table, others jotting down notes on paper. As members of the group take turns speaking, one participant pushes her chair away from the table, folds her hands in her lap, shakes her head back and forth slowly, rolls her eyes upward, and smiles slightly. To others in the group, these body movements and facial expressions might indicate, without words, that this person disagrees with the group's ideas. In addition, the eye rolling and smile may be conveying the message that the person who has pulled away believes the group has impractical or silly ideas.

- A young man and woman stand face-to-face, clasping each other's hands, talking quietly and smiling at each other. An observer would likely assume the two are exchanging messages of affection, since their body language and facial expressions seem to confirm this.

- An umpire and a baseball team manager "face off" during a game. You don't need to hear their voices to know that they disagree with each other. Their facial expressions, the rigid way they hold their bodies, and their arm and hand movements all indicate that an argument is taking place.

On numerous occasions, a person's body movements and gestures help illustrate, like photos that accompany a magazine article, what she or he is saying. Suppose a trainer is introducing a youngster to the sport of amateur boxing, which is almost impossible to learn with words alone. The trainer usually begins formal instruction by explaining how to make a fist, a seemingly simple procedure but one often performed incorrectly, and which can result in broken fingers and other hand injuries.

"Do not twist, bend, or drop your wrist," a trainer might begin. "Form a tight fist by clenching your fingers into the palm of your hand. Fold your thumb across the fingers, forming a flat surface on the thumb side of your hand. Hold your arm and fist straight out in front of you in a rigid line." At the same time the trainer speaks, he demonstrates how to make a fist.

In some instances, nonverbal messages may convey just the opposite of what a person says in words. If you say "I'm really sorry Joanne lost the race," but speak in sarcastic tones and have a smirk on your face, an observer would probably understand right away that you don't mean what you say. Instead you are putting across the message that you are quite pleased Joanne was not a winner.

Although sarcasm often is used to make a point, it is not always the most effective way to communicate what you truly want to say. When your body language and facial expressions don't match your spoken words, the message you deliver can be muddled.

Effective Speech Communication

Former president Ronald Reagan was known as a "great communicator" because he had good command of speech communication skills that were developed during his days as an actor. In a prepared speech, Reagan was able to use voice inflections and deliver words with appropriate timing—pausing or speeding up for dramatic effect—to put across that he was in charge. His voice was pleasant and easy to listen to, and his body language and facial expressions along with a sense of humor showed that he was at ease with himself. According to Roger Ailes, a communications expert who was one of the consultants for Reagan's political campaign, the former president's manner of speaking helped persuade and convince many Americans not only to vote him into office but also to accept his public policy decisions.

In Ailes's view, the messenger *is* the message, which "means that when you communicate with someone, it's not just the words you choose to send to the other person that make up the message. You're also sending signals of what kind of person *you* are—by your eyes, your facial expression, your body movement, your vocal pitch, tone, volume, and intensity, your commitment to your message, your sense of humor, and many other factors. . . . Everything you do in relation to other people causes them to make judgments about what you stand for and what your message is."[2]

Ailes and those in his consulting firm primarily advise politicians, business executives, entertainers, and other public figures, but, along with many other communication experts, they say people from all walks of life can learn to be effective speech communicators. One of the first steps toward that goal is to learn the techniques of good conversation.

Using Conversation to Interact

Essentially, cordial social conversation and productive non-personal conversation (such as on the job) begin with a basic concept: Speech communication is a way to interact with other people. Most people tend to be "social animals"—they need relationships with others, and interactions with other people are part of almost everyone's daily life. People who have already established relationships also have established their particular ways to conduct conversations, so they hardly think about how they relate through their talk. Good friends, for example, may gossip or chat with each other about countless subjects and never once need to analyze how their speech communication cements their friendship.

However, it is not always easy to engage strangers in a conversation so that you can begin a relationship. Conversing well is a learned skill and sometimes is taught as part of speech, public speaking, and interpersonal or human communication courses. How to develop techniques for effective formal and informal conversations is also the subject of numerous popular books and articles, audio tapes, and videos. These materials usually include examples of how to converse in specific situations, such as when speaking to authorities, conversing with strangers at social gatherings, applying for a job, and so on. But the advice can be applied generally, too. Here are some examples:

- Send and receive accurate messages. Know what you are talking about and listen carefully to understand what others are saying.

- If you are speaking, get to the point. Listeners tend to become impatient when a speaker dominates a conversation with information and opinions that do not relate to the subject being discussed.

- Be supportive and courteous, allowing others to speak. After all, by definition a conversation is talk between people and is not a monologue.

- Ask about the other person's life and ideas in order to bring her or him into the conversation. Talk that is constantly about oneself can quickly turn listeners off. On the other hand, if you never talk about yourself, you may give the impression that you are secretive or "too good" to take part in the normal give-and-take of everyday conversation.

- Avoid talk that excludes someone not part of a particular group. If a group includes members of a sports team or a theater club, for example, talking only about the outcome of the latest game or about a theater performance excludes the person who is an "outsider." A group conversation conducted in a language that the "outsider" does not understand also restricts participation.

- Don't offend people with personal criticisms, racist and bigoted remarks and jokes, or crude gossip.

- Be tactful. If criticism is necessary, try to make it constructive, suggesting a positive way to change a situation. Criticize an action, not the person performing the act.

- Be fair. In conversation as in behavior, a variation of the Golden Rule applies: Talk about others as you would have them talk about you.

- Don't meddle in others' affairs, asking about personal matters and business or offering advice that has not been requested.

- Keep your emotions in check, and think before you speak. Angry outbursts, bitter sarcasm, and constant negative attacks on others can quickly turn a conversation into a polarized battleground.

Finally, the basic concept to remember is that a fruitful conversation has to be a considerate, two-way process. It is a way to relate to and include others.

Chapter Three

What's That You Said?

During conversations, discussions, and other speech communication, most people hear what others say, but few really listen. In a recent business conference, for example, two dozen managers took part in an experimental program to test their aptitude on the job. None of the managers had any doubt about their listening abilities, believing they were dutifully attentive whenever Ellen, the testing administrator, spoke. Ellen gave simple, clear, and precise instructions to participants, asking them to write their answers to questions on a separate sheet of paper provided. However, four of the managers wrote their answers on the test itself. When Ellen pointed out the error, the managers said they "didn't hear the instructions." But hearing was not the problem. The managers were capable of aural reception. They had heard the spoken words, but they had not listened to them.

Here's another example. About 30 people attended a party, and during the evening small groups formed and chatted, often engaging in small talk—idle chatter with no distinct purpose. One of the guests was an author of non-fiction books, and while in conversation with one group was asked what he was presently working on. The author began to explain, but soon realized that people were looking away and not offering any type of feedback. So as he was speaking, he decided to find out if anyone was listening to him. He quickly ended his comments with, "This project I'm working on will probably be included in the library on the moon and I'm sure will be read not only by moonbeam creatures but visitors such as Batman and other supernaturals." Nobody exhibited any surprise or responded to his statement. Obviously, no one was listening.

Poor listening habits plague everyone at times, standing in the way of communication. According to experts, most people spend the greatest portion of their waking day listening, but they may grasp only about 75 percent of what they hear.[1] Why? Because there are many barriers to listening. Learning how to overcome those barriers is part of the task of developing effective communication skills.

Why Listen?

Like other communication skills, listening efficiently aids in understanding and in developing relationships. Certainly listening skills are an asset in school, on the job, and in interactions with people in many different situations. Listening skills help you tune in to the world around you— for pleasure as well as information. In the early morning, you may listen to the sounds of birds chirping or traffic rolling past your home, recognizing that these sounds signal the beginning of daily activity. You may attend musical concerts, turn on the radio, or play recordings simply to be entertained or to learn as you enjoy.

Listening is an important part of jobs that range from

air traffic controllers to business executives to news reporters. Counselors and people who answer emergency and hot line telephone calls must have better-than-average listening skills. Being able to distinguish clearly what a person is saying in an emergency or crisis situation may make a difference in whether a caller lives or dies.

If you are a capable listener, you can save yourself a great deal of frustration and wasted time. Have you ever been in an unfamiliar building and had to ask for directions to a specific office or room? Suppose you are told to "follow the hall to the end, go through the double doors, turn right and go down the stairs, turn right again and follow a short hall, and enter the third door on the left. Got it?" Unless you have listened carefully, you could easily forget half the directions before you reach your destination. That could mean retracing your steps to ask for the directions again or spending frustrating moments trying to find the way on your own.

Listening effectively helps keep an informal conversation or discussion running smoothly. When you speak to other people, you usually get some verbal or vocalized feedback along with nonverbal responses such as head nods, frowns, smiles, and yawns. Perhaps as you talk, someone interrupts with "yes, but—" or "don't you think—?" to indicate that she or he wants to speak. When others take their turn, you can encourage them to put their message across with "yes, that's right" or "I agree" or you might have to interrupt when there is a pause in the conversation to disagree. In short, listening is as much a part of communication as verbal and nonverbal messages. But it is one of the most difficult skills to learn.

Obstacles to Effective Listening

Communication experts say most people speak at 125 to 150 words per minute, but the person hearing the words is usually able to process, or analyze, from 400 to 800 words per minute, enough words to fill two or three double-spaced typewritten pages.[2] Certainly there is plenty of time to figure out the message a speaker is delivering. But all the extra time between a speaker's delivery and a receiver's analysis of a message allows for numerous distractions.

Distractions can be external, like a jet flying overhead or loud music playing nearby as people try to speak. But listeners usually are distracted because they do not concentrate on what is being said. They may daydream, letting their thoughts wander aimlessly.

Perhaps you listen to someone talk about the effects of acid rain on trees and forests, and the subject prompts an image of trees, sending your thoughts astray. You might begin to think about a wooded park where there is a fishing stream. Or you might remember cutting up a fallen tree for firewood or planting trees during an environmental project. The possibilities are endless.

Lack of interest in what a speaker is saying is another barrier to listening. If you are not interested in sports car races, you might "tune out" people who talk about the difficult turns on a track or how a driver maneuvers to pull ahead of the pack. Maybe you prefer listening to someone talk about art galleries and museums, topics that might be a turnoff to the racing enthusiast. Like most people, you probably find it easy to listen to someone who is talking about your interests, but it takes effort to concentrate on what you consider boring. Nevertheless, that effort can be worthwhile, particularly when listening carefully helps a person obtain valuable information or appreciation for a different point of view.

Another obstacle to effective listening is assuming to know what a speaker is going to say. Suppose Doug's neighbor, who has a habit of borrowing, comes by and asks if Doug has a ladder.

"Yes," Doug says reluctantly, because he assumes his neighbor wants to use the ladder.

"Do you know—" the neighbor starts to say.

"I think it's in the garage," Doug interrupts.

"Should I go look? I want to—"

"Well, you can, but it's behind a bunch of stuff," Doug interrupts again.

"I thought you might want—"

"I'll have to move stuff to get to the ladder, but I'm busy right now. Can you come back in about an hour?" Doug asks.

"Okay," Doug's neighbor says with a shrug. "I just came over because your cat is up a tree in my yard and doesn't seem able to get down. I thought I could help."

Making an assumption about what someone will say is similar to prejudging another person, which also is an obstacle to effective listening, as well as to many other types of communication. If a listener prejudges a speaker, the judgments and preconceived notions can get in the way of the message.

You might meet a new person at a party and your first impression could be: "What a nothing person. Looks like a jerk. I'll have to make an excuse to get out of here." Chances are your negative thoughts would distort whatever the person has to say, and you would miss the opportunity to meet someone who could be friendly and interesting.

One more obstacle is constantly being on the defensive, ready to attack. Suppose someone begins to talk about a controversial subject such as abortion, or using animals in scientific and medical experiments, or abolishing the death penalty. Another person may have strong beliefs or convictions about these matters. If a listener does not share the speaker's viewpoint, the listener might start preparing counterpoints while the other person is talking. The listener might even think of a comment that will insult or hurt the speaker. With this kind of thought process going on, little effective listening takes place. Part or all of a message may be lost.

A poor self-image also can stand in the way of effective listening. A person with low self-esteem has a tendency to hear put-downs or criticisms where there are none, or accept as gospel the words of authority figures and not respond to or counter those messages.

 Improving Listening Habits

In spite of obstacles, there are ways to improve listening habits. You can begin by resolving to be an active listener. That means being alert and focusing your attention on what another person is saying, whether in a face-to-face or telephone conversation, or in a discussion, or when listening to formal speeches.

In many informal conversations and discussions, you probably have a genuine interest in the people participating, so you automatically attend closely to their verbal messages. You have empathy and therefore feel and experience with them. Sometimes you indicate this with nonverbal messages such as leaning toward a speaker. But even when you are motivated by genuine interest, staying focused requires practice, repeatedly using techniques that can help you concentrate on what is being said.

One method for improving listening techniques is to repeat what another person has said or rephrase the message in a question format, which not only shows that you are interested but also helps you confirm the content of the message. For example: "The new team plays its first game tomorrow, right?" or "Did you say the TV will be fixed by Monday?" Such a technique can be helpful when you talk on the telephone and write down a message for someone else.

Asking a speaker to repeat is another technique to improve listening habits. It is especially helpful when meeting a person for the first time. Although you may have heard a person's name, ask her or him to repeat it, even spelling the name if that will help you recall it later.

Some people are reluctant or unable to reveal their feelings and thoughts. You may be able to detect this by listening for an uncertain tone of voice or hesitant speech mannerisms. Then you can send some positive vocalized feedback ("mmhm," "yes," "what else?") to encourage the other person to speak out.

Then there are those who criticize you or disagree with your views, and your first reaction is to counter with a personal defense. Try to put aside your personal feelings and keep your thoughts focused on the actions or ideas under discussion, separating them as much as possible from you the individual.

While you are talking, you can listen for feedback from others. It may be only a slight groan, or it could be a deep sigh, a loud gasp, or a laugh. Reaction from a listener can tell you whether you need to change content or manner of speaking in order to get your message across.

During a formal speech or class lecture, taking notes is a way to focus on content and prevent stray thoughts. You don't need to jot down detail after detail. Rather listen for and write down the main ideas and points a speaker makes, along with brief supporting data or evidence that you might want to review later.

Keeping an open mind is also important. Perhaps you don't like a person's manner of dress, voice, or presentation. Concentrate instead on the information you receive and listen to all a speaker has to say. The message might include ideas or data that you had not considered before.

Catching Cues

Although being a silent critic can stand in the way of effective listening, developing a "critical ear" can also be an asset at times. Whenever you listen to someone who is speaking to persuade, such as in a political campaign or commercial, you may need to check for various cues in order to separate fact from fiction and decide whether you are hearing the whole truth. When you analyze content, try to determine whether the speaker is

- making generalizations that are not backed up with evidence or facts.

- showing only the positive side of an issue.

- conveying with voice tones and facial expressions that the spoken words are not the entire message.

- citing a testimonial from a well-known person,

rather than factual information, as a reason to support a view or product.

- using scare tactics to convince people that action needs to be taken or there will be dire consequences.

- distorting another person's point of view or ideas.

- presenting opinions as if they were facts.

You might also want to consider whether you are being influenced by a person's voice intonation and manner of speaking. A deep tone of voice and smooth speaking manner can give the impression that a speaker is not only confident but also truthful. Conversely, a raised voice pitch and slow and hesitant speech patterns frequently suggest that a speaker is being misleading. But be alert. You might "read" either speech pattern incorrectly since there is more to any given message than the voice tone or rate of speech in which it is delivered. Studies have shown that listeners who evaluate the content of a speech or a speaker on voice cues alone seldom are accurate in their judgments.[3] A good listener also has to take into account many other nonverbal signals to determine the authenticity of content as well as to decode underlying messages that are being conveyed along with the words one hears.

Chapter Four

Body Language

Clearly, effective speaking and listening are important factors in communication. But experts on human behavior have found that people rely much more on nonverbal messages, including those conveyed with body language and vocalized paralanguage, to determine the meaning of a message. In one study to learn how people perceive messages, researchers found that participants interpreted 55 percent of a message from body language, 38 percent from paralanguage, and only 7 percent from the actual words spoken.[1]

Like other forms of communication, body language has varied components. These include facial expressions; eye contact and movement; head, arm, and hand movements (including touching behavior); body postures and shifts; and the diverse ways people use space. When used, all of these components have an effect on the message a person communicates.

Researchers who study body movement, or kinesics, as it is known, record people's behavior in photographs or on videotapes and analyze everything from body posture to a blink of an eye to a wiggle of a foot. Although the experts may isolate and categorize specific types of body language, they point out that a silent message does not stand alone; it must be interpreted within a particular setting. One simple example is the gesture a hitchhiker uses to "thumb" a ride: fingers closed into the palm and thumb raised. That same gesture has an entirely different meaning when an umpire uses it in a baseball game.

Researchers often analyze nonverbal signals in clusters, or sets of body movements, that fit together somewhat like words in a sentence and provide a more complete message than would be possible with a single gesture or expression. The findings from kinesics research are being applied in a variety of fields. Psychiatrists, social psychologists, social workers, teachers, and many others can use knowledge about body language to help people interrelate. Salespeople, professional speakers, and others may learn how to control their body language in order to improve their communication skills.

Even though it requires a great deal of study to become an expert on body language, anyone interested in effective communication can begin to take note of body cues. Some body language seems to be involuntary—such as facial expressions that relay signals of happiness, sadness, fear, surprise, disgust, and anger. Other body language is learned and includes conventional or coded signals such as raising one's hand to gain attention, and impromptu actions such as tapping the foot to demonstrate impatience or anxiety. Whether automatic or learned, body language can corroborate or contradict what a person says in words. So in order to understand a total message, you need to determine how a person's "body talk" fits with his or her paralanguage and speech communication. Understanding body language can be a help in relationships with family and friends and can be crucial in some job situations.

Eye Movements and Facial Expressions

When people converse, they look at one another's faces more than any other part of the body, hoping to find an expression that will be a communication cue. Because of the structure of the human face, a person could conceivably make more than 250,000 different expressions, according to one kinesics expert, Ray L. Birdwhistell.[2] But only a very small fraction of those expressions have been identified as silent codes or signals that "speak" without words.

Some of those signals are quick nods of the head, eye movements back and forth, eyelid blinks, a raised eyebrow, a furrowed brow, a wrinkled nose, a smile or a pout, or any number of other facial changes, all of which can carry a specific meaning depending on the circumstance. A raised eyebrow, for example, could express surprise or a questioning attitude.

Although many interpretations of facial expressions are possible, some are interpreted the same way around the world. A person who displays a wide smile, for example, almost always conveys a message of pleasure or happiness. But smiles vary, and one researcher claims to have identified more than 1.8 million kinds of smiles that communicate different messages.[3] The messages sent depend on the context and other verbal and nonverbal communication.

Throughout the world people expect facial expressions

to provide silent messages to support or repudiate verbal and vocal communication. However, many people learn to be "poker-faced" on certain occasions. That is, they control their facial expressions in order to conceal their true feelings. People also consciously use their faces to express specific messages, such as deliberately smiling and winking while speaking to show that their words should not be taken seriously.[4]

Eye behavior and facial expressions often convey messages before people speak to one another for the first time. Strangers in the United States first make eye contact, then perhaps smile and nod to indicate friendliness. But most strangers do not look at one another for any longer than a second at a time. They may glance at one another now and again, but in the American mainstream, a look longer than a second is considered rude or a "put-down." If someone stared at you for several minutes, perhaps you'd begin to feel uncomfortable, embarrassed, angry, or afraid. Maybe you'd wonder if the person staring meant to challenge or harm you.

Even people who know each other well seldom look directly at each other for long periods while talking. A speaker may make eye contact for a second but would avoid staring, because that might cause the listener to become defensive or hostile. You've probably noticed that people who argue are apt to stare at one another to show the intensity of their anger or rage.

When adults scold or punish children, they often tell youngsters, "Look at me when I talk to you!" Children might obey the command, but their eyes usually don't focus directly on the adult. Instead, children are likely to "tune out" and their eyes will seem to glaze over or appear "blank."

On the other hand, it is common for someone to look for lengthy periods at another person or an object that appears pleasant to the beholder. A classic example is the seemingly unbroken gaze of a couple in love. Scientific studies have shown that a person's pupils enlarge when one is interested in an object or person, but a disagreeable sight makes a person's pupils shrink.[5]

Yet there are differences in eye contact behavior. Children in some United States cultural groups are taught to drop their gaze when adults reprimand them. To look someone in the eye would be a signal of disrespect and send a defiant message.

In some nations, such as those of the Middle East, adults feel free to look at one another for several seconds or minutes at a time or to look someone up and down. Such eye behavior is not an insult but instead shows appreciation and interest.

Even though people control eye behavior and facial expressions to convey specific messages or to mask their true feelings, they cannot always cover up. Experts in body language have been able to identify facial expressions that sometimes escape a person's control. Called micromomentary expressions (MMEs), they appear involuntarily and last about two-fifths of a second. Researchers have been able to capture MMEs on film, although the expressions cannot be seen unless the film is played back in slow motion. Even though you cannot see such fleeting expressions, you may be subconsciously aware of them. For example, when you have a hunch that a person is lying to you, perhaps that impression comes from a message relayed by an MME.[6]

Signs and Signals

Along with facial expressions, people use many head, hand, and arm movements, or gestures, to transmit messages. Some gestures are formal codes, rather like the hand signals of sign language that hearing-impaired people use to communicate. In other words, people agree on a particular meaning for the gestures and the signals are broadly understood.

People learn coded gestures early in life. During infancy, a child is taught that waving the hand means "good-bye," nodding the head signals "yes," and shaking the head back and forth means "no."

Some learned gestures are routinely used to communicate. A common greeting gesture is the handshake, or in some cases a hug and kiss. In a formal meeting or classroom situation, a person usually raises a hand to gain a leader's attention and permission to speak. Using the forefinger to "stab" the air and make a point is the way many speakers emphasize or call attention to what they have to say. Some gestures are part of ceremonies and rituals. Two familiar ones are the military salute and the head bowed in prayer or respect.

Dozens of gestures are known globally. Applause, for example, signals approval worldwide. If you raise two fingers in a V, most people would recognize the victory or peace sign. A thumbs up sign also is a signal of approval and means "well done" or "good job." Holding your nose with your thumb and forefinger would signify to almost anyone that something stinks or that you don't approve of a particular action.

Still, a great number of gestures used in one country

could have entirely different meanings in other nations, and those variations can affect communication between people. One example that Roger Axtell described in his book about differences in body language around the world is the "okay" signal, forming a small circle with the thumb and forefinger. While people in many countries understand the gesture to mean "everything is okay or fine," the same gesture signifies "money" in Japan and "zero" in France. In dozens of nations ranging from Brazil to Turkey, the gesture insults because it is considered a symbol for the female genitalia, Axtell explained.[7]

In the United States, many different types of gestures convey important messages. The raised hand of a police officer, for example, signals "stop." A bandleader's raised baton indicates that the musicians should get ready to perform. In construction, supervisors often use hand signals to direct workers operating heavy equipment such as a crane or scoop shovel. At airports, the ground crew uses arm and hand signals to direct pilots moving planes onto runways or into parking areas. Stockbrokers, stage managers, and television crews are others who depend on a variety of gestures to send silent messages while they work.

Body Posture

Body posture and position are other important components in the communication process. In the sports world some body movements and positions become coded signals. Team players often signal one another with a variety of different body postures as well as gestures. Players also try to confuse opponents with fake signals. A basketball player might lean forward as if to dribble the ball but whirl and shoot instead. A football player might fake a pass in order to gain an opening to run.

Performers on stage, in movies, and on TV shows also deliberately use posture and body movements to convey messages. If a performer wants to show nervousness or anxiety, she or he might pace back and forth or sit in a chair with hands clasped tightly in the lap. Maybe an actress wants to display scorn or superiority. She might sit upright, tilt her head back, and view the rest of the world from her vantage point: off the bridge of her nose.

Yet when most people transmit silent signals with body posture and position, they are not necessarily aware that they are getting their whole bodies into the act. Imagine a woman and a boy standing facing each other, about a foot or two apart. The woman stands fairly erect and places her hands on her hips, arms akimbo. The young boy stuffs his hands in his pockets, bows his head and lowers his eyes, and shifts his weight from one foot to the other. She could be expressing impatience, frustration, or anger or a combination of those emotions; he could be displaying embarrassment, contrition, and/or displeasure.

The meaning of a single set of body movements can change with the circumstances, however. Consider this scene: A man sits in his home recliner chair, leans back, puts his hands behind his head, with arms out like wings, and smiles slightly. The message is: He's relaxed. But change the setting to an office or school. A man sits in a chair behind a desk and assumes the same position and facial expression. He would put across the message that he is in charge and possibly feels rather smug about his authority.

Understanding how individual body positions reveal emotions and attitudes can be helpful in the total communication process. Perhaps in a conversation, discussion, or public speech, you want to know whether others are listening to you. Experts on human behavior say that people usually tense their bodies when they are listening or watching with interest. That does not mean they are rigid. Rather, people appear to hold a position of "forwardness" or "openness" as they take in what is going on around them. Just the opposite is true when there is lack of interest.

If a speaker is boring, listeners may slouch in their chairs or sit with an elbow on an armrest, head on hand. Some may sit or stand with crossed arms, gazing here and there. By observing this feedback, you may be able to adjust the content or delivery of your message so that it will be better received.

During group or one-to-one interactions, posture may also have an effect on how people appraise each other. In some experiments using videotaping, researchers have found that people tend to take similar postures—such as sitting with a leg crossed, toe pointing in the same direction—when they agree with or like one another. They appear to "echo" each other's behavior. Just the opposite is true when there is no attraction. Some researchers theorize that "echoing" another's posture can be a way to enhance or develop a relationship.[8]

Space That "Speaks"

Along with body posture, the physical distance a person maintains from other people or things also conveys a silent message. Anthropologist Edward T. Hall, who has long studied what he calls proxemics, or the way people in diverse cultures use space, says that humans, like other animals, are territorial. They lay claim to certain spaces and objects within those spaces.

You are likely to see examples of this on a crowded beach. People mark their territory on the sand with a beach chair, or a towel or blanket anchored with personal belongings. Each marked territory says "This is my place," and it would be separated from another's space by an area of surrounding sand.

People use similar strategies in waiting rooms. They may mark their space with jackets and hats, briefcases, luggage, newspapers and magazines, or other objects.

Perhaps you are aware of how you stake out your own space or territory in a classroom. You may have a desk or part of a table assigned to you. If someone occupies that space or clutters it with papers and books, you might become defensive and try to claim your place. Even if places are not assigned in a classroom, it is common for students to lay claim to specific desks or chairs, expecting others to respect their "territorial rights."

Space not only indicates territory. It also shows one's relationship with another person. Most of us learn from an early age to maintain a distance zone that is comfortable for a particular relationship, even though we may not be aware that we are using space in this way. A comfort zone varies according to culture and whether the interactions between people are personal or impersonal, according to Hall. He categorizes the zones as intimate, personal, social, and public.

A person's intimate space, as the term suggests, is usually reserved for only those with whom one shares very close relationships—family members, best friends, lovers. Personal space is a somewhat larger distance zone, perhaps a couple of feet or more, but not out of arm's reach. Social distance is more businesslike and formal and people might stay anywhere from 4 to 12 feet apart. Public distance is the kind of space a speaker maintains before a large audience.

Personal space probably has the most impact on daily communication patterns. Often called a "bubble area," personal space is an invisible sphere. You may be aware of a person's invisible bubble when you stand in a store checkout line or in a line to buy tickets. People keep just enough distance between one another so that their bubbles are intact. If you should move in on another's bubble area, you would soon know it. That person might fidget or express irritation.

How large a person's bubble area is depends on one's personal background and culture. In southern European countries, such as Italy and Spain, people may have small bubble areas, standing close together during conversations, their bodies nearly touching while they speak. But northern Europeans, such as the British and Scandinavians, have larger bubble areas and expect that everyone except intimate family and friends stay several feet away. Americans of northern European background maintain similar bubble areas; they often feel discomfort if someone "invades" their personal space. On the other hand, Americans who are part of southern European cultural groups as well as some African Americans, Asian Americans, and others maintain a smaller bubble area.[9]

Sometimes there is no way to avoid an intrusion on personal space in public places. On crowded buses, trains, and subways, passengers may have to stand or sit with their bodies touching, so they try to protect their intimate space by holding themselves rigid and not making eye contact with strangers. Or, as an airline traveler explained: "The plane was full and I was in the center of a row of three seats, so for the entire flight I had to play the armrest game. For a time, I would place my right elbow on the armrest to keep a distance from the passenger on my right, and I would alternate with the left side. But seldom was I able to maintain *my* space on both sides at once. It was irritating. I felt trapped."[10]

In many social situations, space communicates status, or a person's "place" within a particular social structure. A president, vice president, manager, or other official in a United States company, for example, may have a private office, but other office workers may work at individual desks in one large room. Hall contrasts this use of space with the way Japanese executives operate. They reserve the use of a private office "for meetings with outsiders" and "prefer to work in large open areas, surrounded by colleagues." Hall explains that the Japanese are group-oriented, and by working together in the same area, they can "insure constant interaction and information flow."[11]

Messages of Touch

Some United States business people and government officials study the meanings of spatial cues in other nations so that they can avoid misunderstandings. They also study the way people use touch or avoid touch in communication.

For instance, it is common for businesspeople in the Middle East, the Mediterranean, and Latin America to share an embrace, touch hands, tap a person on the arm or shoulder with a forefinger, walk arm-in-arm, or in other ways use touch to amplify the spoken word during a conversation. Yet touching a stranger may be taboo in many other cultures. Although the Japanese accept close contact in public places, they avoid touching one another during a conversation with a business acquaintance. To cite one example, it would be offensive if a United States businessman threw his arm around the shoulder of a Japanese man.

Koreans, too, are taught to avoid touching a stranger and to lower their eyes when face to face with another person. Direct eye contact and a touch, no matter how casual, usually are considered a kind of sexual invitation. Such learned behavior has caused communication problems for some Koreans who have emigrated to the United States and opened stores or shops. American-born customers reportedly have been suspicious of Korean merchants who do not make direct eye contact. The merchant's practice of putting change on the counter (to avoid physical contact) rather than in a customer's hand has also been misinterpreted; an American may feel insulted.

Generally, people of northern European ancestry follow a don't-touch pattern with strangers, but they may casually touch another person while speaking. A brief touch is acceptable when it is interpreted as a way to emphasize a point in a conversation. But a touch that tarries usually is unacceptable because it conveys a message of intimacy and may be construed as a sexual advance.

In personal relationships, though, touching is often encouraged. Numerous studies have shown that babies who are picked up, rocked, patted, stroked, kissed, hugged, and so on thrive better than those who are seldom touched and held. Infants deprived of touch for long periods can become withdrawn and so unresponsive that they may die, even though they receive proper nutrition and medical attention.

Through childhood many youngsters learn that various kinds of touches convey concern, support, and love. Someone who offers a comforting hug can help ease another's physical pain or hurt feelings. The way people use touch to express caring and concern depends on their personality and what they have learned within their family. Some people may have deep feelings of concern but be unable to reach out. Others easily express caring with touching gestures.

Unquestionably the language of touch is a major part of courtship messages. People convey their feelings with kissing, embracing, stroking, patting, nuzzling, and other types of touching. The silent messages of touch used during courtship are common ways for partners to express commitment to and caring for one another, although intimate touches can also be expressions of sexual desire that may or may not be motivated by "true love."

Some kinds of touches, like other types of body language, are coded signals. If a teacher or coach pats you on the back, you are likely to interpret the signal as an encouraging "do your best." After a competition, a solid handshake or ritualized handshake with many different clasps and grasps, a hearty slap on the back, or a playful punch on the arm usually means "great job!"

Touching is an important part of greeting messages used around the world. Some of the most common welcoming signals in North America are hugs and kisses between friends and relatives and handshakes between strangers or slight acquaintances. American politicians and other public figures know that a handshake—frequently highlighted by placing a free hand over the clasped ones—helps send a more lasting message than one presented in spoken or written words. It is a personal greeting that a supporter or fan may remember for years. Celebrities also receive nonverbal messages from touch. A handshake or touch from a well-wisher expresses admiration and appreciation.

In other nations, however, people may greet one another with far more elaborate touching rituals. A greeting among two men of the Maori tribe in New Zealand, for example, requires that each man nuzzle his nose against the other man's cheek, and Polynesians rub noses together. Men in Latin American countries frequently greet each other with a crushing "bear hug" or with a handshake and a hearty backslap.

Whether we use a coded signal or act spontaneously, the language of touch usually cannot be interpreted in isolation. Even common greeting signals can take on varied meanings, depending on other gestures, facial expressions, spoken words, paralanguage, and so on. As with other types of body language, touching symbols must be seen within the context of the situation and the other nonverbal and verbal symbols being used. All contribute to the meaning of the total message.

Chapter Five

How Appearance Communicates

Along with the many types of verbal and nonverbal forms of communication already described, personal appearance also can impart a message. Consider the kinds of messages conveyed with the costumes worn by such celebrities as Madonna and Cher and most entertainers on musical videos. How would you interpret the image projected by a man with long scraggly hair, wearing a headband but no shirt, his entire torso and both arms covered with tattoos? What is the symbolic message transmitted by someone in a full-dress military uniform?

Whatever you conclude from another person's appearance, "looks can deceive," as an old saying cautions. In other words, the signals you receive can sometimes be misleading. That is a point that many salespeople make by telling this illustrative story:

It seems an elderly woman approached a young salesman in a car lot saying she wanted to buy a luxury automobile. Because the woman's hair was unkempt, her clothing disheveled, and her shoes worn down, the salesman hardly acknowledged her presence. He believed he was wasting his time, since he'd concluded that the woman couldn't afford a car. He mumbled something about seeing his boss and hurried off. Angry about her treatment, the woman went to the car dealer down the street. A few days later, the young salesman learned that the elderly woman was quite wealthy and had been a regular customer. She not only could afford a car but had paid cash to purchase a top-of-the-line luxury automobile from a competitor.

Although many people believe—and rightly so—that individuals should be judged on more than their outward appearance, most people try to enhance or modify the way they look in order to make a positive impression. Or they may alter the way they look because they want to make some kind of personal or political statement. Learning how appearance can convey messages is an important step in understanding the variety of components that can be a barrier or bridge to effective communication.

Clothing as a Form of Self-expression

Certainly the basic function of clothing is to cover and protect the body, and for many people around the world that is the only purpose of most garments. But people in the United States and other industrialized nations use wearing apparel for more than practical purposes. With many styles and types of clothing to choose from, people frequently buy and wear clothes and accessories to make a statement about who they are or what they represent.

Of course, clothing by itself has little meaning. It signals specific messages and becomes a form of self-expression only because people accept that particular kinds of wearing apparel have significance. Designers, manufacturers, advertisers, and fashion consultants have helped determine what types of clothing the majority of Americans consider fashionable and appropriate for various occasions. Articles in newspapers and magazines and features on TV explain and show how people should dress to appear successful or to create a "with it" look.

Perhaps no type of clothing has undergone as many fashion changes and conveyed as many different messages as denim pants, overalls, and jackets. During the mid-1800s, Levi Strauss, a Bavarian immigrant, first designed overalls from brown canvas that he sold to California gold miners who used the rugged material to make tents and wagon covers. Later Strauss made work pants from a material he imported from France. The fabric was dyed with indigo and became known as blue denim.

Strauss found that many California miners, along with other workers in the West such as cowboys, railroad builders, and storekeepers, needed heavy-duty pants, and Levi jeans quickly became popular work wear, constantly in demand. Anyone wearing denim dungarees, as they were called, would be quickly identified as part of the "working class."

By the early 1900s, denim clothing was also popular in the eastern part of the United States. Many farmers and their families wore denim work wear, as did factory employees. When many workers lost their means of livelihood during the economic depression of the 1930s, the denim clothing they wore became a symbol of poverty. But as the economy improved, designers began to use denim to create clothing for recreational wear, selling jeans as part of a western look. Jeans signaled that the wearer could afford to spend time in leisure activities like playing cowboy or cowgirl during a vacation on a ranch.[1]

From the 1950s on, people have worn jeans to project many different kinds of images. One costume of the 1950s was designed to show defiance and included jeans and a leather jacket inspired by Marlon Brando in the movie *The Wild One*. When jeans were worn by so-called flower children and hippies of the 1960s, who protested the social order, the pants were seen as an antiestablishment symbol. But by the 1970s, designers took over and created jeans acceptable for all groups of people regardless of their social and economic status. Depending on the rest of the costume, jeans could suggest a real-life ruggedness, casual life-style, elegant affluence, or steamy sexiness.

While jeans may be one of the most versatile garments used to create an image, many other types of clothing also are used to make a statement. Shoes, socks, sweaters, sweatshirts, jackets, and hats are just a few items that may become means of personal expression. A brightly colored jacket might indicate an outgoing personality, while a somber one might indicate a more reserved nature. A person might wear clothes with a designer label to show that he or she wants to be known for high style and status. Sports fans may show allegiance to a team by wearing hats, shirts, and jackets with their team's colors and logo.

With their dress, members of some ethnic groups in the United States can show that they are part of a particular culture. A colorful dashiki, for example, is popular among African Americans who want to show allegiance to or appreciation for their ancestry and culture. A woman who identifies with the culture of India may wear a sari. During powwows and other ceremonial gatherings, Native

Americans wear clothing and headdresses that signify their tribal heritage.

People also use cosmetics, wigs, scarves, ties, jewelry, sunglasses, and other paraphernalia to adorn themselves and make a statement. A silk tie with a colorful, "wild" pattern worn with a conservative suit may be a way for a man to show that he has a flamboyant side along with his businesslike nature. Someone might wear a Kente cloth, a scarf of colorful woven material from Africa, around the neck not only as a decoration but also as a symbol of community. Sunglasses today are not just to screen the sun from the eyes; shades help create a fashionable costume.

Teenage Clothing Signals

While people in business, entertainment, professional sports, politics, and many other fields use clothing and accessories to impart many kinds of messages, teenagers frequently are the first to adopt particular fashions to express themselves. Advertising and media images have a major impact on the kinds of clothes that are manufactured for and purchased by young people. From an early age, youngsters want to wear brands of shoes, shirts, hats, and other apparel advertised by cartoon characters on popular TV shows and by sports stars or other celebrities. The demand for wearing apparel popularized by the media increases as students go through their middle grade, junior high, and high school years.

But many families cannot afford popular clothing items, so some kids have resorted to stealing and violence to get what they want. News stories have described instances in which teenagers have attacked and severely injured or killed other children, taking their new athletic shoes, jackets, caps, or other wearing apparel, especially items endorsed by sports stars. Such problems in Milwaukee, Wisconsin, have prompted a parent group to set up a campaign against violence spawned by the latest teenage fashions. They urge young people to avoid wearing clothing that others might want to take by force, and have paid for more than two dozen billboard ads around Milwaukee cautioning young people to "Dress Smart and Stay Alive."

Gang rivalry in inner cities also has spawned violence over clothing. Members of street gangs, who wear color-coded jackets and hats that identify their gang affiliation, have shot and killed those who wear the colors of rival gangs. In some instances, young people with no gang affiliation have inadvertently worn the colors of gang uniforms, making them targets for shootings by rival factions.

Clothing identified with gangs has taken a mainstream twist, however. It has become a popular fashion for suburban teenagers and young people in their early 20s. The clothes are designed in the bold colors used by African tribes rather than gangs. Jackets carry insignia of college teams and shirts are imprinted with slogans such as "Stop the Violence" and "Peace in the Hood."

According to a report in the *Los Angeles Times*, high school students are wearing the clothing to "look tough, rebellious, and way cool. But they also want to send a message: They like the gang look but not gang life. Through what they call 'dangerous dressing,' they say they're telling other teens to stop killing each other and come together."[2]

Along with inner city gang styles, other types of attire

are meant to signify not only defiance but also a show of power. Consider the white-robed Ku Klux Klan and the skinhead "look." The Klan has a long history of violent acts against people different from themselves, and the costumes that Klan members wear during meetings and marches symbolize racism, bigotry, and hatred. While the Klan costume certainly has not become popular street wear among young people, the skinhead look has been more readily adopted.

As the name implies, skinheads shave their heads and usually wear military-type clothing and boots. The look has been adopted primarily by those who claim allegiance to hate groups such as the Nazis and Aryan Nations. Although some young people who call themselves skinheads say they identify with musical groups that have nothing to do with violence, the skinhead dress style usually sends a message of racism and bigotry.

Over the years, young people have adopted varied clothing styles to send defiant messages, as is clear from the denim wear messages of the 1950s and 1960s. But today's skinhead and street-gang way of dressing is much more threatening to many adults who fear the hatred and violence associated with it. Some parents believe the clothing will continue to transmit unintended messages and prompt physical attacks. Shoppers, businesspeople, and security guards in malls look with suspicion on kids hanging out in their aggressive style of clothing, and on occasion call for police protection.

Because of concerns that certain clothing styles send negative signals, some California school districts have established dress codes that prohibit such attire as extremely oversize pants and shirts, drooping suspenders, military-type boots, monogrammed belt buckles, net shirts, and bandannas. Even though student groups have protested that such codes infringe their freedom of expression, state courts have ruled that dress codes designed to ensure student health and safety are legal.[3]

The Messages of Dress Codes

Clothing regulations are a matter of controversy in public school systems across the United States, but dress codes are mandatory in many private schools—both sectarian and secular. Some educators believe that a school uniform or standard form of clothing represents discipline and helps create an environment conducive to learning. Students who wear similar clothing are not distracted by competitive efforts to be the "best dressed" or the "most cool" in appearance, educators say.

Of course, dress codes are not limited to schools. In many areas of United States society, people wear clothes that fit established standards, which are stated in written regulations or are unstated but nonetheless accepted. The majority of Americans adopt a particular manner of dress for ceremonies, for example. Although Americans today are more casual about dressing for special occasions than they were several decades ago, many people still wear formal or "dressy" clothing for weddings, funerals, school graduations, religious services, and similar events. Special attire is considered a sign of respect.

Dress codes are also common in business. Company executives, whether men or women, wear tailored suits to signal that they have authority over other employees and also a higher social status. The uniforms of professionals such as police officers, fire fighters, guides, mail carriers, and nurses are a way to foster group loyalty as well as a means by which the public can identify the members of a profession.

Manner of dress may also be mandated by religious doctrine or custom. Some clergy wear ritual garb—robes, scarves, headgear, and other items—that signify their leadership role and respect for religious traditions. People in a religious community may also show respect and adherence to traditions by the type of clothing they wear. For example, the plain clothing of the Amish is designed to show that members of the group reject worldly ways and want to live simple life-styles. Hasidic Jews indicate their strict adherence to ancient Jewish customs with their dark clothing, hats, and hair locks. Shaved heads, distinctive sarongs, and sandals help identify members of the Hare Krishna, a small religious sect, or group. Men who wear turbans may be showing they are devout members of the Sikh religion (of India) or of an Islamic group.

When appearing as a guest speaker, civic leaders, educators, celebrities, and others wear attire to fit a dress code (undeclared but understood) for the occasion—a somber tailored style for a formal speech and perhaps a more casual style of dress for an informal event. If a speaker disregards accepted dress codes, especially for a formal occasion, his or her spoken message may be blocked by listeners who are concentrating more on the speaker's appearance. Effective speakers, like good listeners, know that adapting to a dress code is an important part of getting a message across.

What Grooming Says

Along with dressing appropriately, being well-groomed—neat and clean in appearance—is another important factor in communicating a message during a public speech. It is also crucial during a job interview and can affect how a person is perceived while on the job. A job applicant might wear appropriate clothing, but if she or he appears with disheveled hair and in rumpled clothes, baggy socks, and scuffed shoes, the impression on the interviewer might be that the person not only is careless about appearance but also has little respect for others.

"I don't want some applicant for a supervisory job coming in here trying to look flashy and cool," says a director of a city park department program. "Casual clothing is fine as long as it's neat, but we don't need somebody trying to make a fashion statement—people should leave the dangling jewelry and other fancy stuff at home!"

Others responsible for hiring employees make similar comments. Personnel managers interviewing applicants for office jobs are some of the most particular about an applicant's appearance, even though they may not be aware of it. Both men and women are expected to look businesslike. Clothing, hairstyle, fingernails, the color of one's socks or stockings and style of shoes might be scrutinized.

Research has shown that those who conduct interviews tend to make a decision within the first few minutes after meeting an applicant. In other words, an interviewer's first impression of an applicant is likely to determine whether she or he is hired. And good grooming plays an important role in making a favorable first impression.

Chapter Six

The Written Word

Nonverbal signals that accompany many types of spoken messages can contradict or muddle what someone is trying to communicate. But what about written messages—words on paper or the electronic screen? Letters, memos, messages transmitted by computer and modem hookups, fax, or wire services are primarily verbal. That is, they depend on words to convey a message, so it would seem that there would be little chance for nonverbal signals to garble the message. However, unless you choose appropriate words and put them together in understandable patterns, written symbols will not express exactly what you mean.

Most of us begin to learn the techniques of putting words and sentences together in elementary grades and continue to develop those skills through high school and beyond. Writing skills are necessary for such occupations and professions as advertising, the clergy, law, sales, science, and teaching. But even if a job does not require writing aptitude, good writing skills can be an asset when carrying out commonplace tasks that are part of daily living.

Sending Written Messages

Throughout a lifetime, there are many occasions when letter writing helps a person stay in touch with friends and family members. Letter writing also is a way to obtain information, to lodge a complaint, to make a political statement, or to support a cause.

Political and social activists take seriously the old saying "The pen is mightier than the sword." They participate in letter-writing campaigns in opposition to or in support of various public policies. Many letter-writing campaigns are designed to protest or advocate local, state, and federal legislation. Others are designed to raise funds for civic and environmental projects or to promote religious and political views. One nine-year letter-writing campaign prompted at least 60,000 letters to the United States Postal Service and in 1992 resulted in the release of 29-cent postage stamps dedicated to Elvis Presley.

Although letter writing was once one of the most common forms of personal communication, it has been on the decline for years. During the 1970s, personal letters accounted for 14 percent of the total mail, but that type of correspondence now has dropped to 5 percent, according to a recent study of postal service operations by the United States Government Accounting Office.

The rising cost of first-class postage has been one factor in the decline of personal mail. Another is the preference for phone communication (including fax). Although monthly long-distance and fax phone charges usually add up to much more than postage costs, people frequently opt for the faster form of communication.

Even when cost and speed are not factors and people

choose to get in touch with others by mail, they may use ready-made greeting cards or form letters. A great variety of greeting cards are designed to convey just about any kind of thought or feeling, expressed in humorous or serious, casual or formal, religious or secular styles. Paperback books with pages of prepared letters and postal cards, perforated so that they can be torn out and mailed, are also available. In addition, computer software programs provide templates for greeting cards, thank-you notes, business letters, and political action forms.

Nevertheless, whether you correspond with friends or family or participate in letter-writing campaigns, an original letter can often be the most effective form of communication. If you write what you think and believe, you have a much better chance of affecting a reader or bringing about action. Many government officials say they are more apt to read and take into account the ideas expressed in a writer's own words than those expressed in a form letter. Creating your own personal letters is also one of the most effective ways to develop writing skills.

Developing Letter-writing Skills

At one time, letter writers were advised to "write like you talk." But taking such advice literally could create not only ungrammatical sentences but perhaps pages of nonsense and trivia. People converse in only partial sentences and repeated phrases; they go off on tangents, use clichés, supplement words with gestures, and fill in pauses with vocalizations.

On the other hand, everyday speech usually includes familiar words, which should be used in effective letters. You also can create a friendly, informal tone as well as a more interesting letter when you use active instead of passive verbs in sentences. For example, compare these two sentences:

The computer program was used by the class and was given a top rating. (passive)

The class used the program and gave it a top rating. (active)

By changing to active voice, you can write a direct statement. Rather than "Your story was read by three editors," you might write: "Three editors read your story."

You also can make a letter more friendly and certainly more understandable if you avoid wordiness and get to the point. For example, a letter printed in the *Detroit Free Press* began: "It becomes necessary for me to call your attention to a case of annoyance and danger to which we have been subjected for some time past, and without any efficient effort on the part of the police to meet the case."[1] The letter writer seems more interested in being proper than in communicating. She might have started more directly: "I want to call your attention to a dangerous situation that the police have not yet taken seriously."

Another example is from a letter accompanying a government study: "In the event no utilization of this material is desirable or possible, disposal of it in an appropriate manner is herewith authorized." Translated: "Throw this report away if you can't use it."

Most letter writers do not try to figure out the entire structure of each sentence before putting it on paper. But in order to state your message effectively in written form, you have to think through what you want to communicate. That means deciding what points you want to make or what arguments will support a single proposition. In short, you have to organize your ideas. Then you can begin to write, letting your sentences flow. Later, you can check the preciseness of words and the structure of sentences and revise for clarity.

For practice, you can start by writing a letter to yourself—as if you were writing a diary entry or as though you were addressing a fictional person. Maybe you have a problem and you want to think it through on paper. You can describe the problem, possible solutions, and why a particular solution might work best for you. Such writing may help you find a resolution as well as help you communicate your thoughts and ideas in a logical manner.

Writing letters to request information is another way to practice one's writing skills. If you compare the following three letters written to this author, perhaps you can determine which one was the most effective in generating a response.

1. Dear Ms. Gay:

My name is _____, and I am 14 years old. I am doing a science project on the greenhouse effect. . . . I was wondering if you had any information about the greenhouse effect you could send me?

Right now I am reading your book *The Greenhouse Effect*, which I am enjoying very much. I hope to hear from you soon.

2. Dear Ms. Gay:

I am an eighth-grade student, and I have been doing research on global warming. In your book *The Greenhouse Effect* you mentioned that third-world countries produce much of the greenhouse gases. I would like to know what the third-world countries are doing to reduce the amount of gases released into the atmosphere. I would also like to know why they aren't doing more. . . .

3. Dear Ms. Gay:

I am an eighth-grade student writing a science report on global warming. I would appreciate any up-to-date information you have on global warming. I would also appreciate any information you could give me on the following:

1. What are safe alternatives of energy?
2. What are different types of renewable energy resources?
3. How can changing transportation and agricultural practices help?
4. What are reasonable ways to control global warming?
5. What are the most important causes of global warming?
6. What can students do now to make a difference in the future?
7. A bibliography of current information.

The second letter prompted a quick reply. Why? Because the questions were on *one* specific topic.

Since the writer of the first letter was reading *The Greenhouse Effect,* the request for "any information" seemed redundant—the book should have provided that. In the last letter, most of the writer's questions were precise, but answering all of them would have been tantamount to writing another book or repeating the information in the already published book on the greenhouse effect, or global warming.

Other ways to practice expressing exactly what you mean in written form is to prepare an opinion piece for your local newspaper or an essay or a formal speech. Such writing gives you an opportunity to present arguments to support a cause or to protest a public policy or to state your views on just about any topic that interests you. To effectively present your views, you will need specifics, which support arguments and help relate them to real-life situations.

Twelve-year-old Wilma Amaro of New York used specifics in an essay she presented at a 1990 youth conference sponsored by the United Nations Environment Programme. Young people from around the world gathered to discuss environmental problems, and Amaro chose the topic of water pollution, certainly a broad subject but one she was able to describe with definitive examples:

> I live in a country where not so long ago a river in the state of Ohio caught fire.
>
> I live in a country where the Monongahela River in Pittsburgh was declared a fire hazard.
>
> I live in a city where the body of water between Staten Island and New Jersey threat-

ened to explode . . . from the huge amount of fuel dumped there.

That makes me sad. For me, for you, and for the children I hope to have some day.

Amaro explained that she was also frightened because "my ocean is full of oil, my rivers are full of poison, my lakes are full of acid, and I drink water from a bottle instead of a bubbling spring. I don't want to live this way anymore? Do you?"

She noted that it was time for people to "put a stop to the craziness where water is our enemy. . . . I can't do much, I'm only 12. But I can do SOMETHING, we all can." Then she described what she did:

> A little while ago my class did an experiment with ocean currents—everybody in the Lab School went to Coney Island and threw bottles into the ocean with notes inside to see where the ocean carried the bottles. My bottle floated up on the beach in Sea Bright, New Jersey, where a policeman picked it up and wrote to me. He said his town depended on the beach for its jobs and that bottles like mine stopped people from coming to the beach for fun—it isn't fun to swim with garbage.
>
> I told my teacher . . . who is from Pittsburgh, where the river is a fire hazard, and he told . . . my principal, who is from New Jersey, where the lakes are dying and the ocean threatens to explode. We all made signs saying we were sorry. Then I took a bus to New

Jersey with the signs to apologize to the town
of Sea Bright for all of us. We're not going to
do it again.

What about you?[2]

Wilma Amaro made her point; her message was clear.
She communicated her ideas to youths at the conference
and also to many other people around the world, who were
able to read her essay/speech by connecting electronically
to a United Nations computer conference.

Electronic Communication

Many students today are learning writing techniques—and
the value of this form of communication—through computer conferences and networks. One example is Kids Meeting Kids (KMK), a computer conference designed for young
people who want to go on-line to express their views in writing and transmit them throughout a region or nation or
around the world. KMK allows some 400,000 children, ages
7 to 19, in 140 countries to communicate via computer
hookups. The goal is to use an electronic means of communication and the written form to bring together kids
from different countries, providing a peek into what life is
like in other nations. In addition, young people have an opportunity to work together by sharing ideas on a variety of
issues.

One major project of KMK is to spread information about
and provide greater awareness of children's rights and violence against children, which is rampant worldwide. For
example, information shared on the conference pointed out
the need to urge government leaders in Brazil to bring to
justice members of death squads who are systematically

killing Brazilian street children—nearly 4,000 were murdered between 1988 and 1990. Primarily, though, kids corresponding through KMK are trying to help one another cope with and find alternatives to violence in their own communities, whether that violence is against young people or among them.

A computer network called KidLink also links young people around the world. Odd de Presno, an educator in Norway, originated the network in 1990 for students aged 10 to 15. It was established with the help of coordinators operating a computer science network in Canada and branched out to networks in other countries, including the United States. Today, messages can be sent by home or school computer (with a modem) that connects with a large computer running a special program. More than 260 of these large computers in various countries link with a major computer system at the North Dakota State University in the United States, which is the key conduit for this means of communication.

Each separate computer conference that is part of the KidLink network is designed to promote global dialogue and to encourage young people to get to know "keypals" from other countries. Thousands of students from Australia, Canada, Iceland, the United States, England, Saudi Arabia, Israel, Japan, and from many other parts of the world have participated and shared ideas.

Chapter Seven

Getting Organized

Sharing ideas is one of the most rewarding aspects of interpersonal communication. In many informal situations, you can express your thoughts and opinions or present information in a somewhat haphazard fashion. You might let one idea trigger another, as in this type of chatter: "Look. There's a bat flying around the chimney. Maybe there are more up there. A chimney sweep might be able to find out. I heard chimney sweeping started in England. I know some kids who're going on a tour to England next year. They plan to stay two weeks."

People who know you well understand from past experience what you might be trying to convey. But more formal communication is a different matter. Most of us have little patience with muddled messages—in print or in public speeches.

Suppose you had to decipher this paragraph:

Many scientists believe that vast destruction
of tropical forests could alter global climate.
With plentiful light, warmth, and moisture,
tropical forests nurture a remarkable variety

of ecosystems. The loss of these forests could seriously hinder efforts to control cancer. Indigenous people in the forests are rapidly disappearing also.

Obviously, you would be confused about what the paragraph is trying to convey. Is it about the effect of forest destruction on global climate? About ecosystems in the forests? About controlling cancer with forest products? Or about indigenous people in the forests?

The big job anyone faces in formal writing or speechmaking is deciding what needs to be conveyed and in what order. To effectively present opinions or information, promote a belief or cause, or initiate action, you need to organize your spoken or written message. Organization is, in fact, fundamental if you want to make sure that the information you have to impart is easily understood and that your message conveys what you mean.

Creating an Outline

Suppose you have to write an essay or report or prepare a speech. You have collected your reference materials and need to organize your ideas and information so that they will effectively convey your intended message. To organize simply means to arrange in a particular order, and an outline helps you create an orderly arrangement.

You might think of the outline as a blueprint of sorts—a plan to show how you will build your message. Or you might think of the organizational form as a map, showing where you will start, how you will progress on your journey, and what the ending point will be.

Before you can start an outline, you need to determine what you want to communicate—the basic purpose or underlying theme of your overall message. Perhaps you want to describe what sports car racing is all about or explain what ergonomics is—how engineers design products and places to suit the needs of people who will use them. Maybe you want to motivate young people to volunteer for various civic projects to "make a difference" in their communities. Perhaps you want to present a humorous speech or essay about the superstitious practices of sports fans. You might want to inform people about a centuries-old recycling industry—the scrap metal industry—or explain how mobile homes and recreational vehicles are manufactured.

Once you know the purpose of your speech or essay, you can write down the main points that you intend to put across. For example, the main points you could make to describe the scrap metal industry might be:

1) People have been reusing scrap metal since ancient times.

2) Scrap metal recycling is a multimillion dollar industry today.

3) Preparing scrap metal for reuse is like operating a factory without a roof.

4) Foundries buy scrap metal to melt down for reuse.

5) Manufacturers buy metal produced from recycled scrap to make new products.

6) New products will again become scrap.

Depending on your topic and main points, you can outline your speech, report, or essay in one of several different ways. A chronological pattern such as the scrap metal idea moves from the past through the present to the future.

Another type of arrangement presents a problem and suggests some resolutions. If you want to motivate people to make a difference in their community, you might begin by calling attention to some specific problem or problems, show how a problem affects individuals or a community, what can be done to correct a problem, and how individuals can take action.

In a humorous presentation, your main purpose is to entertain, so you would use a less rigid structure than the outline suggested for explaining the scrap metal industry. You might present a series of anecdotes or events in an arrangement often called a string-of-beads pattern, or you could organize according to certain categories. If you speak or write about the superstitious practices of sports fans, for example, you might arrange your stories according to various team sports (football, baseball, basketball, or hockey), or you might present anecdotes categorized by types of superstitious practices, from group chanting to wearing certain clothing as good luck measures.

Once you determine the format for your outline and the main points you want to stress, you will need to add supporting material. Under each main point, you would list ideas or examples that amplify or bolster it. Maybe you want to show how kids can make a difference in their community and have organized your speech or essay by topics, such as environmental projects, building projects, working with children, and working with the elderly. Under the latter heading you might list these types of programs: providing phone service, organizing an escort service, promoting a living history week, and so on.

Many outlines prepared for class assignments or business purposes are presented formally, using Roman numerals to number the main points and capital letters to list supporting points, with details under supportive statements numbered 1, 2, 3, etc. But no particular format is set in stone—outlines vary according to the subject and the needs of those who use and read them.

Beginning, Middle, and End

Once you have completed an outline, you can begin to prepare your essay, speech, letter, or report. But the task of organizing is not over. If you want to get your message across, your information and ideas must flow logically from the beginning through the middle to the end.

Many writers and speakers begin with statements, questions, or anecdotes that are designed to capture a reader's or listener's attention. Usually these contain clues to what the message is all about. You might decide to prepare a speech or report on tree planting, because this is a much-needed environmental project and is a popular activity in many communities today. You could start with anecdotes about the way people in ancient times honored and even worshiped trees: Long ago, people believed that trees had spirits that could be captured and taken home in the form of wood carvings or that could be called upon to bestow good fortune by "knocking on wood"—the tree trunk. Today, trees are symbolic; they may be planted to honor someone's memory, protected as historical markers, or named as state, community, or school emblems.

The next step might be describing the practical benefits of trees, explaining the varied products from these natural resources, how they prevent soil erosion, act as windbreaks, provide landscaping, help conserve energy, and prevent global warming. Next you could show how trees are destroyed because of urban smog, acid rain, herbicides, and the growth of towns and cities. Finally you could discuss individuals and groups who plant trees and why they do it—frequently to protect the environment but also for symbolic and aesthetic reasons. You might end with a quote from a modern-day tree planter or writer from the past, describing the value of trees, such as these lines from George Pope Morris, an English poet of the 19th century: "Woodman, spare that Tree!/Touch not a single bough!/In youth it sheltered me,/And I'll protect it now."

Chapter Eight

Sifting Through Doublespeak and Half-truths

As you attempt to communicate effectively with others, you may also have to decode messages that are confusing, misleading, or false. People in many walks of life, including some advertisers, business executives, educators, government officials, politicians, military leaders, and salespeople, use language to appear important and authoritative. In addition, many advertisers and politicans are apt to use half-truths, distortions, or various types of doublespeak to present a message that appears truthful or factual but is not.

What Is Doublespeak?

In 1971 the National Council of Teachers of English began the *Quarterly Review of Doublespeak,* edited by English professor William Lutz of Rutgers University. The council published the magazine to protest the way the federal government manipulated the English language. For example, the number of casualties the United States suffered in the Vietnam War, and the Watergate events that led to the resignation of President Richard Nixon, are just two examples of how the government manipulated the language to its benefit. Since its founding, the journal has continued to call attention to people in public life who deliberately use doublespeak, which Lutz defines as language that "makes the bad seem good, the negative appear positive, the unpleasant appear attractive or at least tolerable . . . [and] avoids or shifts responsibility."[1]

In his book *Doublespeak,* Lutz describes several types of language that are forms of doublespeak: euphemisms, inflated words or terms, jargon, and gobbledygook. You have probably heard or read euphemisms—that is, terms that attempt to make the unpleasant or offensive more acceptable. For example, a garbage dump may be renamed a "waste disposal site," and sewage becomes "sanitary waste." In similar euphemistic fashion, a tax increase becomes a "revenue enhancement," a used car becomes a "preowned automobile," a janitor becomes a "building maintenance worker," a teacher becomes a "learning facilitator," and a salesclerk becomes a "company representative."

Inflated language is a way to appear authoritative, to impress a reader or listener. Consider these instructions for using a personal luggage carrier with elastic cords that hold suitcases in place: "Extreme caution should be taken when cords are stretched. Ends of stretched cords should be held firmly and fastened securely. Care should be taken that face and other vulnerable body parts are kept away from potential cord rebound path." The warning in simple terms is: "Be careful when you stretch the cords. Fasten the cords securely, or they might snap back and hit you."

Jargon, or special language that professional groups use, is another kind of doublespeak used to impress others. For example, someone might say, "I found it difficult to determine what motivational factors caused Terry's actions."

Translated, that means: "I don't know why Terry acted that way." The term "motivational factors" suggests that only an expert in psychology can understand Terry's actions—even though in truth Terry might have acted on a whim.

One more type of doublespeak is gobbledygook, or the use of many words to say little or nothing. This notice affixed to a plastic cutting board is a prime example: "[The] manufacturer has made no affirmation of fact and has made no promise relating to this plastic sheet which has become any basis of a sale or transaction which has created or amounted to an express or implied warrant that this sheet would conform to any affirmation or promise, and disclaims any warranty of merchantability of fitness of this sheet for any particular purpose whatsoever."[2] Apparently, the manufacturer would not correct any problems that might occur with the cutting board.

Gobbledygook frequently appears in business reports, letters, and announcements. One report, written by a company official after inspecting a branch office in a distant state, began this way: "To the extent rendered possible by the limited amount of time allotted to the investigation of this area, it appears generally that assignments and work schedules were, in large measure, being carried out in accordance with desirable standards." Perhaps the message could have read: "As far as I could tell in the two hours that I spent at the office, employees were doing competent work and completing it on time."

Another example is this notice sent to federal employees: "All appropriate personnel shall endeavor to give full compliance to the regulations therein promulgated." If the words had been more direct, the meaning would have been clear: "Everyone must follow the rules."

An announcement that a university administrator sent to staff described intentions "to reduce our utility costs by reemphasizing common sense conservation measures. If a change in the interior environment becomes noticeable, personal attire modifications can be used to compensate and achieve a proper level of comfort." Apparently, the university intended to reduce air conditioning and wanted the staff to wear cool clothing when necessary.[3]

In still another example, a vocational school administrator sent a memo to shop teachers, describing what steps they should take to prevent student injuries and possible lawsuits. It began: "To set forth all-inclusive examples of conduct and responsibilities vocational education teachers should observe to avoid judgments in court is impossible. However, it is generally agreed among authorities on school law that teachers are likely to be considered negligent under the following circumstances, should an accident to a student occur." The administrator could have written: "Shop teachers should take the following precautions to avoid lawsuits for negligence."

Many politicians speak in gobbledygook, and former Vice President Dan Quayle's remarks frequently fit the category. In 1990, while speaking about the federal role in education, he said: "Quite frankly, teachers are the only profession that teach our children. It is a unique profession and, by golly, I hope that when they go into the teaching field that they do have that zeal and they do have that mission and they do believe in teaching our kids and they're not getting into this just as a job or a way to put food on the table." Many who heard Quayle shook their heads and wondered what he meant. Was he praising teachers or criticizing them? Was he saying that teachers should have a "holy" purpose and that they should expect low pay for their professional work?

When doublespeak is baffling, humorous, or pompous, it seldom causes much harm, but jargon and gobbledygook frequently deceive people. Thus learning to identify doublespeak can help you separate partial truth or lies from messages that communicate honestly.

Doublespeak and Half-truths in Advertising

Most people are well aware that print ads and TV commercials are designed to show goods and services in the best possible light so that consumers will buy. Nonprofit organizations also promote their causes through advertising in order to gain support. So it is usually no surprise that advertisers use euphemistic terms and inflated language in their sales pitches or that nonprofit groups present only their side of an issue in promotional efforts.

In ads for products and services, the most common forms of doublespeak are euphemisms and inflated language. As Lutz pointed out in his book:

> In the world of advertising, people wear "dentures," not false teeth; they suffer from "occasional irregularity," not constipation; they need deodorants for their "nervous wetness," not for sweat; they use "bathroom tissue," not toilet paper; and they don't dye their hair, they "tint" or "rinse" it. Advertisements offer "real counterfeit diamonds," without the

slightest hint of embarrassment, or boast of goods made out of "genuine imitation leather" or "virgin vinyl."[4]

Some common types of inflated language that appear on a variety of products include names with terms such as "plus" or "ultra," which suggest that a product is of the highest quality. Goods for sale may be described as "new and improved," "more absorbent than ever," "better quality," and "more nutritious." Such terms suggest quality products, but how do you know what "improved" means? Against what and whose standards is the product being compared? What measurements or guidelines do you use to determine whether one product is "better" or more absorbent, nutritious, or whatever than another?

Ads not only make use of inflated language but also present partial truths. For example, in some supermarkets, you might see a sign in the fresh produce section that declares: "Our produce is lab-tested for pesticide residues." Such a claim has little meaning unless you also know what kinds or what amounts of pesticides—chemicals used to kill pests on fruits and vegetables—are hazardous to your health if left on produce. You would also need to know whether the laboratory that performed the tests is reliable.

An example of another more subtle use of half-truth is part of an antiabortion TV commercial sponsored by a foundation that supports primarily evangelical Christian causes. It shows a variety of scenes with healthy, happy children laughing and playing, while a commentator's voice says: "All of these children have one thing in common. All of them were unplanned pregnancies . . . that could have ended in abortion. But their parents toughed it out, listened to their hearts and discovered . . . that sometimes the best things in life aren't planned." The commercial ends with the words: "Life. What a Beautiful Choice." It leaves the impression that all of the 1.8 million aborted pregnancies each year in the United States could have been brought to term and result in happiness ever after. Yet the fact is that thousands of unwanted children are born annually and that many of these children will be neglected, physically and sexually abused, and perhaps even killed by their parents.

Other types of TV commercials promote such causes as enlistment in the military, describing the opportunities for travel and education but not the dangers of armed combat. Or commercials tout the benefits of nuclear power but do not mention the problems and dangers of storing highly radioactive nuclear waste. There is not space here to describe the varied ads and commercials that show only part of an issue. You can, however, ask questions about any type of advertising or promotion. Is it misleading? Are important facts being left out? Is it stating only partial truths? Does it contain meaningless terms? Do some statements prompt only an emotional response and not a thoughtful assessment of the message? The latter question is one that many citizens need to ask when they hear or read messages from government and military officials.

Government and Military Doublespeak

In general, Americans seem to expect government officials to distort the language and to say and write things that they don't quite mean. But some people compare the practice to "Newspeak," a language used in George Orwell's prophetic novel *1984*, published in 1949. In Orwell's fictional police state, called Oceania, the government presented lies as truth, indoctrinating people with such slogans as "war is peace," "ignorance is strength," and "freedom is slavery."

Although most people believe they are able to distinguish between such distortions of truth, they may not be aware of the many ways in real life that their government and military leaders manipulate language to avoid unpleasant reactions or to gain support for an unpopular national policy. One example is calling a deadly missile—a weapon of war—a "Peacemaker." Troops trained for war are called "peacekeepers." An invasion is a "rescue mission." And civilian deaths are "friendly casualties" of war.

When military leaders speak in public, few ever talk about bombing and killing people but instead refer to "ordnance" and the "collateral damage," as if an exploding bomb blows up only buildings and equipment. During the Persian Gulf War in 1991, generals appearing on TV shows frequently talked about KIAs rather than speak of soldiers killed in action. The term, as one columnist in *Maclean's* described it, "lends a disconnected, neutral air to things. [KIAs] are not dead soldiers, they are inventions of the alphabet and therefore not something we have to deal with." In short, such language evades the truth and manipulates citizens to think of war as a game or TV show.[5]

Every political campaign prompts a great outpouring of gobbledygook. Politicians may stress such terms as "family values," "law and order," "free enterprise," "investment in America," "welfare reform," "educational excellence," "the American dream," and "the cultural elite." These terms, and countless others like them, do not have specific meanings, but politicians use them because they prompt emotional responses.

During the 1992 presidential campaign, for instance, people attached many shades of meaning to the term "family values," used over and over again in speeches. To some people, the term meant that the idealized family structure—father as wage earner and mother as care giver—should dominate today, and that people should pattern their lives according to that ideal. But that family structure is no longer common in the United States (and never was for poor families who could hardly survive without the income that women earned). Thus to many people, the term "family values" became a codified way to condemn such family structures as two wage-earner parents working outside the home, single-parent families, stepfamilies, and families with two parents of the same gender.

Some candidates (and those who write their political speeches and press releases) deliberately use doublespeak to avoid taking a stand on an issue or to duck responsibility for some governmental action or personal behavior. For example, when the United States Congress voted a pay raise for members, one congressman explained the action as a "pay equalization concept." After President George Bush supported a raise in taxes in spite of his famous read-my-lips-no-new-taxes pledge, Congressman Newt Gingrich defended the president by insisting that Bush "explicitly didn't say 'raise taxes.' He said, 'Seek new revenues.'"[6]

"Political Correctness" In Language

For at least a decade, another type of language, politically correct (PC) language, has been a controversial topic on university campuses, in textbook publishing, and in the news media. Although there is no exact definition for "political correctness," it is generally the use of language that shows sensitivity to those who are different from oneself. The intent is to help eliminate prejudice by avoiding the use of language that offends others.

There is little doubt that many terms that are part of the English language are offensive, such as ethnic and racial slurs and insults aimed at people's sexual orientation. Such language usually stems from attitudes of superiority and stereotypes of groups not part of the dominant society.

Some terms and phrases have become so much a part of "common talk" that they appear acceptable to those who use them, but they certainly are insulting to those who are being stereotyped. Consider just a few offensive remarks: "Jew them down" suggests that all people who practice Judaism haggle, and that haggling is a negative trait. "Drunk as an Irishman" implies that all people of Irish ancestry drink to excess. Terms like "redskins," "brave," "squaw," and "papoose" are condescending and stereotypical ways to describe individuals of Native American ancestry.

Racist and bigoted language not only perpetuates prejudice and false ideas, it also leads to violence. Name-calling, ethnic slurs, and stereotypes reinforce prejudice and hatred, which in turn prompt some individuals and groups to bomb homes and businesses and to beat and kill those different from themselves.

In some instances, efforts to enlighten the public about the destructive effects of racist, sexist, and bigoted language have helped to change attitudes. People in many walks of life today are aware of and celebrate America's diversity and understand that its culture has been created not by one but many ethnic groups.

Indeed, most PC language is designed to replace terms that suggest "inferior" status for members of minority groups and terms that exclude women, older people, and those with handicaps. For example, it is politically correct to use the term "people with disabilities" but not "the disabled" or "disabled people." The latter terms suggest that a particular group of people are inferior in some way to the majority in society, while the PC terms apparently show sensitivity and are thus are not considered put-downs.

"Indigenous people" is the PC way to categorize people native to a land, and "people of color" is the PC term for anyone who is not Caucasian and of western European origin. To avoid sexist language, "humankind" and "members of the human race" are PC replacements for "mankind," and "manufactured" is a replacement for "man-made."

Some universities and publishing companies have created long lists of PC terms to replace those that are considered offensive. In some cases, various terms are banned, such as "glamorous" because it is considered sexist, "ugh!" because it is an example of stereotyped Native American speech, "mafia" because it is offensive to Italians, and "community" because it implies that people think and act the same way.[7]

In the view of some critics of political correctness,

efforts to use "sensitive" terms have become what Mortimer B. Zuckerman, editor-in-chief of *U.S. News & World Report*, calls "a bizarre version of Orwellian Newspeak."[8] For example, people with disabilities may become "people who are differently abled," which to many people seems highly inflated language. Another inflated term is "nontraditional age students," considered a more sensitive term for "older" students.

Some have called political correctness "a totalitarian philosophy," citing several instances when students or faculty attempted to bar free speech and inquiry because various terms would be offensive to certain groups of people. PC language can intimidate students, educators, and others who attempt to present controversial ideas. Some are afraid to make any critical statements about any group in society because they may be labeled racists or bigots and accused of being discriminatory. Such fears can stand in the way of effective communication—on or off campus.

Yet on a broader scale, there is no doubt that racist and bigoted attitudes are widespread in the United States, and when those attitudes are expressed in words and symbols, they create some of the most formidable barriers to effective communication. Perhaps PC language will help in some small way to change prejudicial attitudes, but it is more likely that communication barriers will be broken down primarily by people on an individual basis—by those who truly want to communicate.

Chapter Nine

Overcoming Roadblocks to Communication

Since communication is the means we all use to establish relationships with others, most of us want to overcome roadblocks to communication so that we can interact and relate. Applying some of the communication skills described in previous chapters can help you create and develop a new relationship or maintain rewarding relationships with family, friends, classmates, and co-workers.

In addition, it is important to be aware that people use many different styles of communication, which can sometimes obstruct or muddle messages. By understanding some of these variations, you can more easily communicate with individuals whose ideas, background, and culture differ from your own, as well as with people you know well. Other major obstacles to effective communication include personal conflicts and anxiety about social interactions. These, too, can be reduced or overcome—if people are willing to make the effort.

Differences in Style

The way people communicate sometimes depends on gender and communication patterns that were learned while growing up. But no one way of communicating is better than another. One type of communication style might fail in one situation but work well in another. For example, a person who habitually asks a lot of questions during a discussion may be annoying to a group, but that same person might do well on a research project that requires a great deal of one-on-one interviewing and inquiry. In another example, if you have been taught to take your turn and not interrupt during group conversations, you may get upset if you meet a group of people who feel it is okay to talk before someone else finishes. You may have to adapt your style to the group's. Because it is expected, you may have to break in whenever you can to get your message across.

Frequently, as is clear from observations of the way people use body language, most of us convey indirect messages and do not always say what we mean. Although Americans in general expect people to be honest and direct in what they say, the truth is that honesty can sometimes be unkind and that directness may make a speaker appear rude, manipulative, or even cruel. Would you, for example, tell a person directly about his or her bad breath, body odor, or some other unfavorable trait? Unless you knew the person well, you might find a way to put the information across through hints or by describing the problem in terms of someone else.

Honesty and directness might not be appropriate in another kind of situation. Would you say to a boss or other person in authority "I don't like the way you give orders"?

Or would you find some less direct way to signal that you don't like being treated in a high-handed manner?

In her best-selling book *That's Not What I Meant!* linguist Deborah Tannen explains that people receive benefits from indirectness—they can show sensitivity to other's feelings, they can protect themselves from negative reactions, and they can feel good about being understood without using specific words. In Tannen's view,

> through indirectness, we give others an idea of what we have in mind, testing the interactional waters before committing too much— a natural way of balancing our needs with the needs of others. Rather than blurt out ideas and let them fall where they may, we send out feelers, get a sense of others' ideas and their potential reactions to ours, and shape our thoughts as we go.[1]

If, however, you expect directness from others, you may be impatient with someone who is indirect, perhaps drawing the conclusion that the person is devious or "wimpy" or untruthful. So you might easily misunderstand a message. The trick is: While interpreting a message, be aware of differences in communication style and how that style might affect what is being conveyed verbally and nonverbally.

Cultural patterns also affect one's style of communication, as Thomas Kochman, a professor of communication at the University of Illinois at Chicago, has found in his studies. Kochman has concentrated on differences between black and white styles of communication and how they sometimes clash.

In general, Kochman describes the communication style of whites as restrained and controlled and characterizes black style as "a willingness to contend" or to struggle and become involved. According to Kochman, whites generally see struggle and contention as negative, and believe that

> if people are too involved and too intense, it's likely to produce confrontation. Better not to struggle at all. They say: "I can't talk to you now, you're too emotional.". . . For blacks the refusal to contend is withholding and cheating, and it demonstrates an unwillingness to get at the truth.[2]

As a result, whites see blacks who are involved in an emotional discussion as being argumentative and militant, while blacks see whites who strip emotion from their presentations as uncaring and cold. In short, the two different styles create barriers to communication. But Kochman insists that these need to be discussed even though some people believe that talking about differences is a form of racist behavior, because behavior different from the accepted pattern is often regarded as negative. But differences are not negative or positive. They simply are—and need to be understood in order to bring about effective communication.

Differences in personality and personal problems may also affect one's communication style. Nancy, a data processor in a business office, explained how she first established a relationship with Julie, a co-worker, who appeared negative, unfriendly, and at times rude. Although Nancy was outgoing and made friends easily, her efforts to start a conversation with Julie "never seemed to go anywhere."

Nancy explained how that changed when "one day, during lunch hour, I shared part of a low-calorie dessert with Julie. I explained how I was trying to deal with a weight problem—a problem I knew Julie was struggling with, too. When I told her about my ideas for losing weight, she wanted to learn more. Eventually, we decided to work together, to support one another in exercise programs and a low-calorie diet. From then on, we learned to trust one another and to communicate about other important aspects of our lives. It turned out that Julie had little self-esteem, but as she began to lose weight she also began to like herself. And she became a more courteous and friendly person in the office."[3]

Conflict Resolution

Because people communicate in different ways, their varied styles can lead to conflict. But conflicts also stem from many other causes and are part of daily living. Every family, for example, at some time experiences conflicts between its members. Those conflicts may come about for a variety of reasons. Members of a family may not share the same goals, or some members may have values different from other members, or some members may not agree with family rules or may not want to be part of the family.

Various groups in a society also have conflicts because their goals and priorities differ and their methods for achieving goals may clash. Conflicts develop when people compete for a limited number of jobs or natural resources, when some groups feel their ways are superior to those of other groups, or when people's religious beliefs differ.

Whatever the reasons for conflicts, some can have destructive consequences, as news stories of beatings, stabbings, shootings, and other violence so tragically show. But conflicts can also have constructive effects, such as helping people to explore new methods for relating to one another and accumulating new information. In order to minimize the negative aspects of conflicts and emphasize the positives, experts in human behavior spend a great deal of time developing ways to help people manage conflicts peacefully and lessen stress that leads to conflicts.

In personal relationships, conflicts frequently are the result of poor communication, whether between family members, friends, classmates, co-workers, or others with whom one comes in contact on a regular basis. Myriad counselors and self-help books and tapes discuss ways people can resolve conflicts through communication techniques, which vary according to the type of conflict and specific situation. But you can apply a few general guidelines:

1. Talk about differences and problems whenever possible, using a reasonable and calm tone of voice. (Controlling the pitch and loudness of your voice might also help you control and organize your thoughts in order to present them objectively.)

2. Avoid the "silent treatment"—nothing is gained if you refuse to communicate.

3. Try to clarify reasons for conflicts without making accusations; reject name calling, insults, and unflattering comparisons. (How would you feel if you were the recipient of this message: "You

stupid idiot! You made a mess of things! You ought to be more like. . ."?)

4. Be a nondefensive listener; let the other person express her or his feelings or viewpoints without interrupting to present your side of the argument.

5. Resist statements with "should have," "could have," and "ought to have," as in "You should never have done that!" The deed is done, so nothing is gained by belaboring past actions; deal with the present.

6. Use problem-solving techniques, identifying the nature of the conflict and who is most upset about a problem, discussing possible solutions, and implementing a solution that is acceptable at least in part to everyone involved.

7. Accept responsibility for your own ideas and feelings; speak only for yourself—say what you feel or think—not what you believe another person has in mind.

8. Try to accept situations that cannot be changed or that are beyond your control, such as mishaps from the past or other's ethnic or religious background.

9. Experiment with different styles of communication if one method doesn't seem to work.

10. Get help if communication breaks down and conflict escalates; find a mediator, someone who will help both sides look at conflicting views objectively.

Coping with "Communication Apprehension"

What is "communication apprehension"? First, it is in itself an example of inflated language, an academic term for anxiety that inhibits communication. People who are anxious about communicating with others are usually shy.

According to communication experts and psychologists, everyone experiences shyness on occasion. Surveys in the United States and several other countries "suggest that at least 30 percent of young adults everywhere consider themselves too shy. More than 70 percent say that at some time in their lives shyness has hampered them socially."[4] In one survey of college students, between 10 and 20 percent suffered "severe, debilitating communication apprehension." That is, students were unable to function because of their anxieties over communicating with others.[5]

People who are shy about communicating in social situations frequently are uncomfortable when meeting strangers. They may be nervous or tense in group discussions and be afraid to express themselves. Some may be tense and even feel sick while giving a speech. Rather than experience such traumas, some shy people try to avoid social gatherings or meetings in which they will attract attention and be expected to communicate publicly. They may also shun occupations that require public speaking and many group encounters.

Some communication experts theorize that people develop anxieties about communicating with others early in life. Perhaps they feel inadequate in some way and judge themselves too harshly; they may believe they will be rejected because they do not meet others' expectations. People who have had little opportunity to learn social and communication skills—how to act, dress, converse—in a variety of social situations usually feel anxious about the kind of impression they will or do make. If after a social encounter they believe they behaved awkwardly or were unpopular, then their self-esteem suffers, reinforcing their anxieties. In the next social situation, their feelings of inadequacy persist and the cycle continues. But a person can break the cycle and reduce or overcome shyness and anxieties not only by applying communication skills but also by learning how to relax and think positively.

The relaxation technique may be as simple as taking part in physical activities, such as walking or jogging, to help free the mind and reduce tension before a social situation. It is also relaxing to be familiar with a situation. If, for example, you are starting a new job, you would try to learn as much as possible about your duties, co-workers, the location, and so on. If you know what to expect, you are much less likely to be anxious about facing a "strange" situation—it seems familiar or known to you.

Another relaxation technique—muscular relaxation—requires practice. British psychologist Peter Trower explains:

> To use it, construct a list of the situations that make you anxious, from easiest to most difficult. Then imagine as vividly as possible the least difficult situation, and allow all of your muscles gradually to relax one by one, starting from the tips of your toes and the tips of your fingers until you reach the muscles of your face and neck. Allow yourself to feel as

though you are floating in space. This re-
laxes away the anxiety that the image brings.
You then go on to the next situation. By prac-
ticing it is possible eventually to reduce the
anxiety that the real-life situation habitually
brings.[6]

One part of the muscular relaxation technique is
changing negative habits. If you consistently think of yourself in negative ways, you may have programmed yourself
to fail. But replacing negative thoughts with positive ones
can be constructive in almost any situation. If you can focus
on success, think of yourself in a positive light. You are
more likely to function effectively when you communicate
with others.

Chapter Ten

Putting Communication Skills to Work

Undoubtedly there will be many significant occasions as well as ordinary instances during your lifetime that will require use of effective communication skills. Meeting new people, applying for a job, resolving conflicts with family members or friends, working cooperatively with a group, and acting in a leadership capacity are just a few instances in which you could be called upon to put some communication skills to work.

Following are some real-life situations that require effective communication. As you read them, determine what could be done to overcome barriers to communication, get a message across, and establish or improve a relationship.

> Barbara had just moved to a midwestern town and hoped to get acquainted with two teenage girls—twins—who lived next door. But the first time Barbara tried to greet them outside their home, the twins started to whisper to each other. As Barbara moved toward them, she heard one of the twins say, "That's the new girl from the East. She . . ." Barbara didn't stick around to hear any more. Immediately, she whirled and ran across the street. Because the

twins were obviously talking about her, Barbara decided at once that the girls disliked her, so she avoided any contact with them.

Jason applied for a job as a bagger at a supermarket. He was ten minutes late for the interview. When he arrived in a rush, he explained to the store manager that his car had had a flat tire. Jason said that he had changed the tire and that he had not had time to wash up. He didn't realize that he had a streak of grease across his face and dirt on his pants. As he stood talking to the manager, Jason kept one hand in his pants pocket, jangling his car keys and change. The manager finally said he was sorry, but he would have to cut the interview short. He'd call later to let Jason know whether he was suitable for the job.

Donalee's grandmother came to visit from another state. The grandmother had never met Donalee's boyfriend, Bill, so Donalee invited Bill to join them one evening for dinner. When Bill arrived at Donalee's house, he mumbled a greeting and nodded "hello" to Donalee's mother and grandmother. But Bill told Donalee he couldn't stay—he had something important to do. He left almost immediately. Donalee's mother and grandmother both expressed anger and disgust; they felt Bill had been inconsiderate and rude. Donalee became defensive and refused to comment during dinner.

Although there are no perfect solutions to improving communication in these three situations, here are some possibilities: Barbara could try again to make contact with the twins and might find out she had misunderstood the verbal and nonverbal messages she received from them; perhaps the girls had been discussing how they could approach Barbara, hoping they could become acquainted. Jason could have called the store manager to explain his problem and make another appointment for a job interview, which would have given him the opportunity to appear on time in clean, neat attire. Donalee might have provided some type of explanation for Bill's behavior rather than sitting in sullen silence.

Being an Effective Communicator

Whatever types of communication skills you might apply in a specific situation, you can use those skills to your advantage if you think of them as social tools; they can help you relate to strangers, develop friendships, and maintain close relationships. Many different factors influence the messages that you convey, but you can use the following A to Z summary of skills as a guide:

Acknowledge responsibility for your own behavior and communicate "I messages"—what *you* think and feel.

Be true to yourself, communicating honestly and conveying the truth as you see it.

Convey respect for other's ideas; don't monopolize a conversation or discussion.

Disagree without being disagreeable.

Empathize with others.

Feed back verbal and nonverbal messages to encourage other speakers to share their views.

Give praise when it's due, but don't overdo with gushing insincerity.

Hone your writing skills by keeping a daily journal or diary or by writing letters to friends and relatives.

Increase your ability to interpret contradictory spoken messages by looking for body language or listening for paralanguage cues that do not support spoken words.

Join a drama club, debate team, or similar group to help develop communication skills.

Keep your distance if you observe that a person with whom you are speaking has a large "bubble area."

Learn how people of cultures different from your own communicate so that you can avoid misunderstandings.

Monitor your own verbal and nonverbal messages at times to determine ways you can improve your communication skills.

Note and apply communication skills that others use successfully.

Organize and outline the main points you want to convey in a speech, essay, or report.

Paraphrase another speaker's words and ideas to

make sure you understand the content and meaning of a message you heard.

Question the messages of those who use double-speak, and distinguish between fact and inference.

Respect others' private disclosures; don't pass on others' secrets as gossip.

State your views and ideas in a concise manner; stick to the point.

Talk to other people the way you would want them to talk to you.

Use active voice whenever possible in written reports and essays.

Vary your communication patterns, particularly in conversations, balancing active listening with speaking.

Write thank-you notes to those who provide helpful services, present gifts, or in other ways act on your behalf.

X-out offensive racist and sexist language, and avoid stereotyping and labeling others.

Yell only in appropriate situations, such as shouting for emergency help or expressing excitement during an athletic event; turn down your voice volume in one-to-one or group discussions.

Zero in on mixed messages; try to identify them in others and to control mixed signals in your own messages so that you convey exactly what you mean.

. . .
. . .

Notes

Chapter One

1. Edward T. Hall and Mildred Reed Hall, *Hidden Differences: Doing Business with the Japanese* (Garden City, New York: Anchor Press/Doubleday, 1987), p. 3.
2. Henry Sampson, *History of Advertising* (London: Chatto & Windus, 1933), p. 19.
3. Ron Scherer, "Learning Lessons Long-Distance," *The Christian Science Monitor* (November 4, 1991), p. 14.
4. Bill Barnhart, "What Keeps Good Jobs Unfilled," *Chicago Tribune* (January 5, 1992), p. 10.
5. Quoted in Philomena Jurey, "Innovations: Getting the Message Across," *The Washington Post* (January 23, 1991), p. B5.

Chapter Two

1. Peter Marsh, ed., *Eye to Eye: How People Interact* (Topsfield, Massachusetts: Salem House Publishers, 1988), p. 107.
2. Roger Ailes with Jon Kraushar, *You Are the Message* (Homewood, Illinois: Dow Jones-Irwin, 1989), p. 20.

Chapter Three

1. P. Judson Newcombe, *Communication: An Introduction to Speech* (Newton, Massachusetts: Allyn and Bacon, 1988), p. 61. Also J. Regis O'Connor, *Speech: Exploring Communication* (Englewood Cliffs, New Jersey: Prentice-Hall, 1988), p. 53.
2. Florence J. Wolff, Nadine C. Marsnik, William S. Tacey, and Ralph G. Nichols, *Perceptive Listening* (Englewood Cliffs, New Jersey: Prentice-Hall, 1983), p. 154.
3. Marsh, *Eye to Eye: How People Interact,* p. 108.

Chapter Four

1. Marsh, *Eye to Eye: How People Interact,* p. 47.
2. In Roger E. Axtell, *Gestures: The Do's and Taboos of Body Language Around the World* (New York: John Wiley & Sons, 1991), p. 10.
3. Ibid., p. 60.
4. Philip Emmert and William C. Donaghy, *Human Communication* (Reading, Massachusetts, and Menlo Park, California: Addison-Wesley Publishing Company, 1981), p. 171.
5. Joseph A. DeVito, *The Interpersonal Communication Book* (New York: Harper & Row, 1989), p. 237.
6. Ibid., pp. 234–235. Also Emmert and Donaghy, *Human Communication,* p. 171.
7. Axtell, *Gestures: The Do's and Taboos of Body Language Around the World,* p. 101.
8. Marsh, *Eye to Eye: How People Interact,* p. 59.
9. Edward T. Hall, *The Hidden Dimension* (New York: Anchor Books/Doubleday, 1969), pp. 113–129.
10. Personal interview.
11. Hall and Hall, *Hidden Differences: Doing Business with the Japanese,* p. 12.

Chapter Five

1. Iain Finlayson, *Denim: An American Legend* (New York and London: Simon & Schuster Fireside Book, 1990).
2. Michael Quintanilla, "Looking Bad," *Los Angeles Times* (March 6, 1992), p. 1E.
3. Jon Nalick and Rose Apodaca, "Schools Making Anti-gang Statement with Dress Code," *Los Angeles Times* (July 28, 1992), p. 1B.

Chapter Six

1. Susan Watson, "A Gracious Writer Becomes Indignant," *Detroit Free Press* (February 19, 1992), p. 1B.
2. "Statement of Wilma Amaro," unep.nyu.youth computer conference, January 29, 1991, available on Econet.

Chapter Eight

1. William Lutz, *Doublespeak* (New York: HarperCollins, 1990), p. 1.
2. "Selling It," *Consumer Reports* (June 1991), p. 447.
3. Quoted in Jack Smith, "Clearly, It's a Plastic Language with Devious Overtones," *Los Angeles Times* (October 24, 1990), View section, p. 1E.
4. Ibid.
5. Allan Fotheringham, "The Word They Dare Not Speak," *Maclean's* (February 18, 1991), p. 56.
6. Quoted in Smith, "Clearly, It's a Plastic Language with Devious Overtones," p. 1E.
7. Charles J. Sykes, *A Nation of Victims* (New York: St. Martin's Press, 1992), p. 6.
8. Mortimer B. Zuckerman, "The Professoriate of Fear," *U.S. News & World Report* (July 29, 1991), p. 64.

Chapter Nine

1. Deborah Tannen, Ph.D., *That's Not What I Meant! How Conversational Style Makes or Breaks Your Relations with Others.* (New York: Ballantine Books, 1986), p. 80.
2. Quoted in Connie Lauerman, "Do You Hear What I Hear?" *Chicago Tribune* (November 5, 1985), section 5, p. 1. Also Thomas Kochman, *Black and White Styles in Conflict* (Chicago: University of Chicago Press, 1981), pp. 58–59.
3. Personal interview.
4. Daniel Perlman and Peter Trower, "Coping with Shyness," in Marsh, *Eye to Eye: How People Interact*, p. 23.
5. DeVito, *The Interpersonal Communication Book*, p. 137.
6. Pete Trower, "Thinking Anxiety Away" in Marsh, *Eye to Eye: How People Interact*, p. 187.

For Further Reading

Adler, Mortimer J. *How to Speak, How to Listen: The Pleasures of Conversation*. New York: Macmillan, 1983.

Practical advice on how to prepare lectures, speeches, and sales talks and how to develop listening skills is the major emphasis of this book.

Ailes, Roger with Jon Kraushar. *You Are the Message*. Homewood, Ill.: Dow Jones-Irwin, 1989.

Communication expert Ailes shows how people send messages about who they are with facial expressions, mannerisms, speech patterns, and many other verbal and nonverbal signals.

Axtell, Roger E. *Gestures: The Do's and Taboos of Body Language Around the World*. New York: John Wiley & Sons, 1991.

The subtitle aptly describes the type of anecdotes found in this amusing, illustrated book, which covers over 200 gestures used in 82 countries.

Fast, Julius. *Body Language*. New York: M. Evans and Company, 1970.

This is one of the earliest books explaining in nonacademic terms the science of kinesics and how people use space, facial expressions, touch, gestures, and other body language to communicate.

Gabor, Don. *How to Talk to the People You Love*. New York: Simon & Schuster, 1989.

Writing for teenagers in a straightforward manner, the author explains how to "combine coolness with compassion, logic with understanding, affection with discipline and trust with openness" in personal communication with friends and family.

Hall, Edward T. *The Hidden Dimension*. New York: Anchor Books/Doubleday, 1969.

An anthropologist introduces the science of *proxemics*, a term coined by Hall, in this book on how the use of space can affect relationships and interactions between people.

Hall, Edward T. *The Silent Language*. New York: Fawcett World Library, 1959.

Although written decades ago, this definitive work still provides a clear explanation of how people "talk" to one another without using words.

Kochman, Thomas. *Black and White Styles in Conflict*. Chicago: University of Chicago Press, 1981.

Written for college students studying communication techniques and laypeople as well, this book shows how black and white cultural differences affect styles of communication and should be understood in order to reduce or prevent conflict.

Lutz, William. *Doublespeak*. New York: HarperCollins, 1990.

In this popular book, the author shows in easy-to-understand terms how doublespeak can be amusing but is also a way for those in power to consciously use "language as a weapon or tool...to achieve their ends at [others'] expense."

Marsh, Peter, ed. *Eye to Eye: How People Interact*. Topsfield, Mass.: Salem House Publishers, 1988.

Abundantly illustrated with color and black and white photographs, this large-format book portrays and explains the great variety of ways that people communicate and interact with one another.

Newcombe, P. Judson. *Communication: An Introduction to Speech*. Newton, Mass.: Allyn and Bacon, 1988.

This textbook for high school students covers far more than speech communication, including sections on listening skills, interpersonal relationships, and nonverbal messages.

Powell, David. *What Can I Write About?* Urbana, Ill.: National Council of Teachers of English, 1981.

Written primarily for teachers, this practical guide and listing of 7,000 topics is useful for junior high and high school students who need ideas for research and reports, descriptive essays, critical and comparative writing exercises, and creative writing assignments.

Reisner, Robert. *Graffiti*. Chicago: Henry Regnery Company, 1971.

Arranged chronologically, the anecdotes in this book show how graffiti scribblers over the centuries have expressed diverse sentiments, ranging from anger and hope to wit and wisdom.

Rosetree, Laura. *I Can Read Your Face*. New York: Dell Publishing, 1990.

Based on the author's experiences and drawing on her "own intuition," as she put it, this book outlines theories for reading faces, although none have been scientifically tested. In an informal manner, the author explains how facial features, from eyebrows to the chin, reveal certain character traits.

Tannen, Deborah. *That's Not What I Meant! How Conversational Style Makes or Breaks Your Relations with Others*. New York: Ballantine Books, 1986.

Although this book deals with the academic field of linguistics, it clearly shows how age, personality, ethnic and class background, and where one lives can affect conversational style.

Index